Writing Paragraphs

Writing Paragraphs

Carol Pemberton

Normandale Community College

Allyn and Bacon

Boston   London   Toronto   Sydney   Tokyo   Singapore

Executive Editor: Joseph Opiela
Production Administrator: Rowena Dores
Editorial-Production Service: Editorial Inc.
Text Designer: Pat Torelli
Cover Administrator: Linda Dickinson
Manufacturing Buyer: Louise Richardson

Copyright © 1991 by Allyn and Bacon
A Division of Simon & Schuster, Inc.
160 Gould Street
Needham Heights, Massachusetts 02194

Library of Congress Cataloging-in-Publication Data

Pemberton, Carol A. (Carol Ann), date
   Writing paragraphs / Carol Pemberton.
     p.   cm.
   Includes index.
   ISBN 0–205–12715–0
   1. English language—Paragraphs. 2. English language—Rhetoric.
I. Title.
PE1439.P388   1991
808'.042—dc20

90–44070
CIP

This textbook is printed on
recycled, acid-free paper.

Printed in the United States of America
10 9 8 7 6 5 4 3 2   95 94 93 92

Credits

Page 4–5. Excerpt from "The Price of Human Folly," *Discover,* April 1989, p. 75. Jared Diamond © 1989, Discover Publications.

Page 8. Reprinted from *Lowell Mason: His Life and Work,* copyright © 1985 by Carol A. Pemberton, with permission from UMI Research Press, Ann Arbor, MI.

Credits continued on page 256, which constitutes an extension of the copyright page.

Contents

Preface

Writing Paragraphs is designed to help students master basic composition skills. The book is focused on paragraphs because paragraphs are brief enough to be managed conveniently, yet long enough to afford practice on the universal principles of prose writing.

Because the paragraph consists of a general statement supported by specific statements, I begin by stressing the distinction between general and specific. In the opening chapter I also introduce paragraph unity and development. In Chapters 2 through 5, I guide students to consider audience and purpose, discover and narrow topics, shape topic sentences, build support, and ensure coherence.

Beginning with Chapter 6, I present narrative, descriptive, expository, and persuasive paragraphs in separate chapters. As students read, analyze, and write paragraphs of these various types, their understanding of audience and purpose, unity, development, and coherence is reinforced.

Though I focus on individual paragraphs as a convenient means for teaching principles of composition, I also encourage students to examine the paragraph's role in more extended passages. In the last chapter I deal explicitly with multiparagraph units, but on many other occasions as well, I guide students' consideration of passages consisting of several paragraphs. Throughout the book, I help students to see paragraphs from both internal and external perspectives.

Because good writers must be critical and analytical readers, I emphasize analytical reading in every chapter of this book. For the most part, students' work is used for analysis because those examples are more meaningful to beginning writers. In some instances I annotate passages to draw attention to specific features. Elsewhere I ask students to read sample paragraphs, then to discover their main features by answering leading questions.

Supported by annotations and study questions, the sample paragraphs show students how other writers have worked to attain unity, development, coherence, and organization. By reading carefully, keeping in mind the principles they are studying, students find the strengths and weaknesses in the sample paragraphs. Thus, besides supporting the text commentary, the sample paragraphs encourage critical evaluation. The paragraphs also stimulate class discussion, particularly when it is directed toward ways of improving those paragraphs. As students grow accustomed to critiquing sample paragraphs in the text, they become more comfortable in criticizing one another's writing and their own.

Each chapter ends with exercises designed to sustain students' interest and to offer teachers flexibility. The exercises are widely varied. Some require short answers; some demand narrowing of overly general statements, shaping of topic sentences, revising of sentences for coherence, or grouping of ideas for paragraphs; others involve analyzing or revising of paragraphs. Every chapter includes at least one exercise in which students are asked to write paragraphs on suggested topics, topics of their own choice, or topics assigned by the teacher.

When I used the manuscript in my classes, I found that as students moved through the chapters, they became adept at selecting and refining topics, building support, ensuring coherence, and organizing logically. For revising and proofreading, they referred to the checklists in Chapter 10. Because I do not address questions of grammar, sentence structure, usage, and spelling in this book, students need access to handbooks and other reference works.

Writing Paragraphs lends itself to collaborative work among students and to peer evaluation. The sample paragraphs can be used to demonstrate features students should consider during peer evaluation and while revising their own work. As students learn more about the principles of good writing, they will become better readers as well as better writers.

Acknowledgments

Over the years, many of my students have agreed to have their writing reproduced in my textbooks. On behalf of the readers of this book, I wish to thank these students for their contributions to *Writing Paragraphs:*

David A. Appel, Bryan Bademan, Sue Bard, Lillian C. Blaine, Wade Boelter, Kathy Braaten, Kristin Brey, David M. Carlson, Andrew B. Crawford, Tore Dahle, Sandra Dalby, Pat Donahue, Jerry Elliott, James Erler, Lois R. Freed, Kristen Fritz, David Funk, Shelly Gaspar, Lance Gerling, Tom Grendahl, Jeff Guelich, Kaytee Hanson, Tim Heiland, Debbie Hennes, Kris Kaeding, Steven Kampen, Bob Kos, Barbara Lafontaine, Charlotte Landwehr, Tracy Leask, Bob Liegl, Leanne Mandelkow, Danielle McCullough, Mike Merritt, Chris Miller, Mihai Miu, Monika Morris, Christopher C. Nelson, Julie Nelson, Scott Niznick, Sandra Olberding, Duane O'Loughlin, Jim Pemberton, Xoua Pha, Joel Phyle, Daniel Pommerenke, Joel Prest, Joan Purdie, Rob Rogers, Chris Salmon, Brenda Salseg, Bruce

Schuette, Carla Schulz, Dan Sweeney, Angela Taylor, Kraig Vanden-Branden, Sandra Wagner, Andy Way, Jill Weinand, Brett Wetterlin, and Jim Wombacher.

Many teachers of writing reviewed the manuscript and offered valuable suggestions: Michael Hennessy, Southwest Texas State University; Eric Hibbison, J. Sargeant Reynolds Community College; C. Jeriel Howard, Northeastern Illinois University; Douglas Krienke, Sam Houston State University; Daniel L. Miller, Northern Kentucky University; Audrey Roth, Miami-Dade Community College; Judith Stanford, Rivier College; and Katharine Stone, Georgia State University.

I am indebted to the Allyn and Bacon staff and particularly to my editor, Joe Opiela, for his insight and guidance throughout the preparation of this work.

Finally, I am grateful for the patient support of friends and family.

Writing Paragraphs

1

Reviewing Basic Concepts

Looking at Paragraphs

When you hear the word "paragraph," you may think of a block of printed matter on a page. You might expect the first line of that block to be indented five spaces or about a half inch, like this:

Xxxxxxxxxxxxxxxxxxxxxxxxxxxxxxxxxxxxxxxxxxxxxxxxxxxxxxxx
xxxxxxxxx. Xxxxxxxxxxxxxxxxxxxxxxxxxxxxxxxxxxxxxxxxxxxxxxxxx.
Xxxxxxxxxxxxxxxxxxxxxxxxxxxxxxxxxxxxxxxxxxxxxxxxxxxxxxx
xxxxxxxxxxxxxxxx. Xxxxxxxxxxxxxxxxxxxxxxxxxxxxxxxxxxxxxxxxxxx.
Xxxxxxxxxxxxxxxxxxxxxxxxxxxxxxxxxxxxxxxxxxxxxxxxxxxxxxx
xxxxxxxxxxxxxx. Xxxxxxxxxxxxxxxxxxxxxxxxxxxxxxxxxxxxxxxxxxxx
xxxxxxxxxxxxxxxxxxxxxxxxxx. Xxxxxxxxxxxxxxxxxxxxxxxxxxxxxxx
xxxxxxxxxxxxxxxxxxxxxxxxxxx. Xxxxxxxxxxxxxxxxxxxxxxxxxxxxxxxx
xxxxxxxxxxxxxxx. Xxxxxxxxxxxxxxxxxxxxxxxxxxxxxxxxxxxxxxxx
xxxxxxxxxxxxxxxxxxxxxxxxxxxxxxxxxxxxxxxxxx.

As a reader, you know the paragraph at a glance, just by its appearance. Ordinarily as you read from paragraph to paragraph in longer pieces of writing, you pay little attention to individual paragraphs. If you pause to notice, you will see that paragraphs vary considerably in length.

Practice 1-1.   Finding examples of paragraphs

DIRECTIONS: *Open a book other than this textbook and count the paragraphs you find on any three pages.*

1. What is the name of the book? _____

2. How many paragraphs did you find in three pages? _____

3. How many paragraphs do you see per page, on the average? _____
   (Four to six is the typical number.)

4. Select one page and read it carefully. Can you tell why the author started

   each new paragraph? _____

   _____

   _____

As a reader, you have learned that paragraphs are more than a visual block on the page. You know that the sentences grouped into a paragraph deal with the one main idea in that paragraph. As you read from paragraph to paragraph in a piece of writing, you move from one main idea to another. Together, a series of paragraphs develops a larger, more complicated idea. Each paragraph explores that idea and helps readers understand it.

Paragraphs include **general** and **specific** statements. General statements provide a broad view of a topic. Consider this general statement:

> Even though I had pretty good pay, working in that factory was a terrible job.

Readers can interpret "pretty good pay," "working in that factory," and "a terrible job" in many ways. The writer must provide specific details. What was the pay? What was the job? What was terrible about it?

Sentences like these give specific support for that main idea:

- The pay was $11.55 an hour.
- The job was boring; all day I was grinding and polishing metal to make car doors smooth.
- I stood on my feet all day, every day, for eight hours.
- The factory was always smelly and noisy, with hundreds of machines running all the time.

As this example shows, a general statement provides only an assertion about a "terrible job." To understand what the writer means, readers need specific statements that include exact information. In the next examples, some words are underlined in the general statements. Then, in the specific statements, the underlined words are replaced with exact information:

General: Many popular television programs are situation comedies.
Specific: A television program with high ratings during the 1980s was "The Cosby Show."

General: Caffeine can be harmful.
Specific: Too much caffeine can disturb sleep and cause irritability.

General: The desert has a harsh climate.
Specific: On the desert, daytime temperatures often exceed 100 degrees, and there is no protection from the blazing sun and hot wind.

Practice 1-2.   Creating specific statements

DIRECTIONS: *Write specific statements that give details about these general statements. Invent any details you need:*

Example

General: Recent studies show that this city has a sizable Hispanic population.

Specific: According to the 1990 census, 17 percent of this city's residents are Hispanic.

1. *General:* The intersection near my apartment house is dangerous.

   Specific: _____

   _____

2. *General:* Construction workers put in long, hard hours.

   Specific: _____

   _____

3. *General:* My sister is a fine athlete.

Specific: _____

_____

If you compare your answers in Practice 1-2 with those of your class-mates, you will find many kinds of responses. That diversity is to be ex-pected because readers interpret general statements in different ways. Writers need both general and specific statements. The specific statements are particularly important, however, because they let readers know exactly what the writer means. In paragraphs, general and specific statements are needed for these reasons:

- General statements summarize the main ideas of paragraphs.
- Specific statements focus readers' attention on specific features of the main ideas.

A good paragraph leaves readers with clear understanding because one main idea has been explained specifically. The sentence stating that main idea is the **topic sentence**. That sentence makes an assertion or a claim that needs explanation in other sentences. The topic sentence can be the first sentence in the paragraph. When it is, readers find out immedi-ately what the paragraph is about.

The other sentences in the paragraph need to be more specific than the topic sentence. These sentences support the topic sentence by giving facts, examples, definitions, illustrations, and other kinds of explanation. Writers use many kinds of support, and each must relate to the main idea clearly and be helpful to readers.

Sometimes a paragraph introduces ideas that are discussed in greater detail in later paragraphs. The sample paragraph below comes from the middle of a magazine article about the ill-fated expedition led by British explorer Robert Scott, who died in 1912 in Antarctica. The writer begins this paragraph with a general idea, then gives somewhat more specific ideas in support. Later in the article, the writer goes on to discuss each of his statements still more specifically. Notice, however, that even here the paragraph moves from a general statement at the opening to more specific statements in the rest of the paragraph:

topic
sentence ⎰ All leaders of expeditions into unexplored areas have
              ⎱ faced the same set of interpersonal problems. The leader must

one   get <u>the most from his followers, often under unpleasant and</u>
problem   <u>dangerous conditions</u>, but <u>must not drive them to the point of</u>
              <u>collapse or mutiny</u>. There is a fine line between motivating

another problem

a third problem

people so that they give their best and manipulating them so that they feel deceived. Furthermore, many expedition members possess <u>specialized knowledge that the leader lacks and requires.</u> A leader must know not only how to give orders but also how to elicit and evaluate advice. Hence <u>there is another fine line to recognize,</u> between honest and dishonest advice.

—Jared Diamond, "The Price of Human Folly," *Discover,* April 1989, 75.

All writers must decide how general to be and how specific to be—and keep a reasonable balance between general and specific statements. The length of the piece of writing makes a big difference. The writer of the paragraph above wrote several more paragraphs to explain how Scott motivated his followers, how he gave orders, and how he reacted to advice from others. When writers have many paragraphs to work with, they can handle larger, more complicated general ideas.

When time and space are limited, writers trim down the generalizations and get into specific support at once. Too often, inexperienced writers start with overly large generalizations. Then it is impossible to support those ideas adequately.

In the sample paragraph below, a student writer sets out to discuss a topic just as dramatic as an expedition in Antarctica, but this writer uses only one paragraph to express his ideas. Notice that the writer offers mainly general statements without support:

topic sentence?

too obvious

Is it comparable to varsity sports?

Some people <u>really thrive</u> on excitement. They think <u>it</u> makes them feel more alive. One form of pure excitement can be found in the <u>sport</u> of skydiving. *sport?* This sport involves jumping from an airplane with a parachute. The amount of excitement I get from skydiving is surpassed by no other, in my opinion, and I *how much excitement?* have been in a number of varsity sports all through school. Nothing is quite like the <u>thrill</u> of jumping and falling. It is true <u>excitement.</u> *Why? What do you mean?*

As a reader, you would ask many questions about these statements, questions such as those in the margin. This paragraph gives very little

information about skydiving. The writer says that skydiving is exciting and
a thrill, but he never does explain what is exciting or thrilling about the
experience.

Practice 1-3.   Analyzing an overly general paragraph

DIRECTIONS: *The paragraph below was written by a student. She began
with her topic sentence. All the other sentences should explain the topic idea.
Consider each of the other sentences carefully. Underline the sentences that
are too general to explain the topic idea.*

topic sentence (During my four years in the United States Army, I discovered what kind of person I am. I found that I didn't have any
problems working with people I didn't know. I found that I
can remain calm and clear-headed under stressful situations.
Even under the worst situations, I was able to find humor to
boost my spirits. I learned that honesty is better than lying,
even if I was in the wrong; therefore, I have become more
comfortable and at peace with myself. During my tour of duty,
I endured some bad experiences in relationships and work. I
found that no matter how bitter the experience, I would re-
cover. I have established self-confidence that gives me the de-
termination to accomplish my goals. After being assigned
projects to do on my own, I have found that I enjoy my own
company and can do a good job.

*If you could talk to this student, you might ask her how she found humor
in "the worst situations." What other specific details would you ask for?*

1. _____

2. _____

3. _____

The examples above show why specific information is vital. Without it,
readers do not know what you mean about the thrills of skydiving or about
discovering "what kind of person I am." The more complicated or unfamil-

iar the main idea of a paragraph is, the more readers rely upon specific information. It is the writer's task to select appropriate information and arrange it in ways that help readers understand.

Introducing Unity and Development

One quality of a good paragraph is **unity.** When applied to paragraph writing, unity means that the paragraph is about one primary idea; all the statements in the paragraph have to do with that one idea. The writer does not wander away from the idea, but rather stays with it and leads readers to a clear understanding.

Unity comes from clear, well-worded topic sentences and specific supporting sentences that back up the topic sentence. In the paragraph you read in Practice 1-3, all the sentences do pertain to the stated topic. Those sentences are so general, however, that they give almost no information.

By contrast, read the paragraph below, in which a student explains his interest in coin collecting. The main idea is stated in the opening sentence. Notice how exact the supporting information is. Supporting ideas are marked:

topic sentence

For most of my life I have been fascinated with coins. As <u>far back into my</u> childhood as I can remember, I <u>recall</u> <u>looking at coins, handling them,</u> and reading the dates on them. I started collecting coins when I turned seven, and I've been collecting them ever since.

tells when, what he did

shows others noticed his serious interest

When my family saw how serious my interest was, my dad bought me coin-holder books, and my grandpa gave me his entire collection. As a teenager, I saved money from my weekly allowance and my paper route so that I could buy more coins. With each purchase, I wrote down

tells what he did

shows how he kept records

the name of the coin, its date, condition, and type. Now I have a valuable collection with about 500 coins. My oldest coin is a 1798 large cent penny, and my two newest

tells what he has

shows his current interest coins, which are contained in a set, are 1988 proof silver one-dollar and half-dollar commemoratives. To this day, when I have time, I go to the bank and buy rolls of pennies, nickels, or dimes, and search for rare coins. *shows his goals* My immediate goal is to build a collection of about 1,500 coins over the next five years. Eventually I hope to pass along my interest and my collection to children of my own.

Practice 1-4. Finding unity in a paragraph

DIRECTIONS: *In this paragraph, the topic sentence is the first sentence. The entire paragraph is about the beauty of the city. As you read the paragraph, underline all the ideas that support the topic sentence:*

topic sentence   The city of Savannah, [Georgia], one of the most inviting of American cities for a newcomer [in 1813], offered many attractions, beginning with <u>its beauty</u>. Neat, pale yellow brick houses lined the sidewalks. *a main idea in the paragraph* Many homes were surrounded by walled gardens in which giant live oaks, garlanded with Spanish moss, provided shade. The fragrance of flowers perfumed the wide, tree-lined streets. Pioneer Governor James Edward Oglethorpe (1696–1785), one of Savannah's founders, had ensured that many plots of land were reserved for parks. In these areas magnolias, azaleas, palmettos, and other semitropical vegetation have flourished to this day.

—Carol A. Pemberton, *Lowell Mason: His Life and Work* (Ann Arbor, MI: UMI Research Press, 1985), 10

Another quality of a good paragraph is **adequate development**. The paragraph should include enough specific details to explain the topic idea thoroughly. The more complex or abstract that topic idea is, the more details and explanation the reader will need. Paragraphs of only two or three sentences usually don't give a reader enough details. But even if the paragraph has six or eight (or more) sentences, the reader will not understand your message if those sentences are too general. You saw in Practice 1-3 an example of overly general statements throughout the paragraph; consequently, you found it hard to understand that writer's point. General statements will not provide a good understanding, but six or eight specific supporting statements will generally serve that purpose.

Most of the sentences in your paragraphs will be supporting statements. A typical paragraph follows this pattern:

opening (the topic sentence)

supporting sentence
supporting sentence
supporting sentence
supporting sentence } many sentences
supporting sentence (no particular
supporting sentence number)
supporting sentence

ending (conclusion or restatement of the topic idea)

To develop your paragraphs, you must include relevant, specific, detailed information in the supporting sentences. The paragraph about coin collecting is a good example. The writer mentions specific times in his life, the current and target size of his collection, and the date and description of his oldest coin. Those specific details give a reader a clear understanding of the entire collection.

In this paragraph, a student begins with a topic sentence, then explains with details:

topic sentence

The time and effort I spent on becoming a scuba diver have been well worth it. In 1989, I enrolled in a forty-hour training course to become a certified scuba diver. The course consisted of twenty hours of classroom study and twenty hours of training in the water. The classroom hours gave me technical

tells what she did, type of training

explains her fears and how she over- came them information about the equipment, physical conditioning, and safety procedures. *explains the training*
Then came the hard part, the scary part.
I had to get into my gear and train in the
water. The instructor had fifteen years of
diving experience, but she still remembered how scared beginners can be. She
was patient, but firm. She helped me
overcome my fears and develop some
confidence. By the end of the course, I
was certified as a scuba diver. Since then I
have gone diving in the cold water under *explains her enjoyment of the skill*
the ice of Minnesota lakes and in the very
warm waters of the Caribbean Sea and in
many dive places in between. Completing
the scuba-diving course was not easy, but
it certainly was worth all the effort to me.

Practice 1-5. Finding specific support

DIRECTIONS: *In the student paragraph below, the topic sentence is the first
statement. Underline the sentences that you believe are most useful in supporting the topic idea.*

topic sentence   I learned early in life that I had to be more patient and
less aggressive. From the time I was about four years old until I
was about six, I was a destructive person. My parents bought
me toys, and I was happy as long as the toys worked. But when
things went wrong, I got frustrated and angry and sometimes
broke the toys. For a while my parents bought new ones, but
before long they began to see what was happening. On my
fifth birthday they bought me an electric train set. Within a few
weeks I smashed it because a short in the wiring had cut the
power. My parents said, "That's it! No more toys for you for a
long time." About a year later my punishment ended. Mean-
while, I found out that with more patience I could make my

toys last. I found out that I had fewer problems with things breaking. My attitude changed from then on.

General and specific statements are stressed throughout this book. As you have seen, specific statements are especially important because they convey exact information to readers. Unity and adequate development are also emphasized in the chapters ahead. These qualities are considered separately for our convenience, though in fact they work together.

General and specific statements, unity and adequate development in paragraphs—these concepts may seem overwhelming at first. Remember that no one writes clear, specific information in unified, well-developed paragraphs just by knowing some rules. At the same time, though, all writers need to know the goals and keep them in mind as they write.

Writing takes patience and practice. Writers erase a lot. They make false starts and throw away lots of paper. They stray from their topics. Then when they look at what they have written, they have to throw away those irrelevant statements. Most writers start with general ideas, then refine and change those ideas, making them more specific. They add, subtract, and alter their supporting ideas.

You can begin by letting your ideas flow freely. Simply write, filling several pages. Then go back and look at what you have written. See which statements are general and which are specific. See if you have wandered from your topic. Find your main idea. It may not be the first statement you wrote. You may have discovered a strong, worthwhile idea as you went along. Perhaps you developed that idea instead of the one you began with.

As you work on paragraph writing, pay attention to the paragraphs you read. Notice the arrangement of ideas in paragraphs you find in books, magazines, and work-related documents. Look for unity and development of main ideas. You will see that these principles apply in paragraphs and in longer pieces of writing as well. As you move through this book, you will find that writing well-developed, unified paragraphs is more easily said than done. Still, with practice, you can get good results.

Throughout this book, you will be looking at students' examples. You will examine them for their strengths and weaknesses. You have looked at some examples already, and the exercises below give you more to analyze. By examining the work of others you will develop the ability to analyze and improve your own work.

Summary

- A paragraph is printed as a visual block on the page, set off by indenting the first line.

- A paragraph is a group of sentences that conveys one main idea.
- Specific supporting information is essential in building good paragraphs.
- The main idea of a paragraph is given in a topic sentence.
- Other sentences in the paragraph support the idea expressed in the topic sentence.
- A good paragraph has unity and adequate development.
- Unity means that all the sentences relate to the primary idea expressed in the topic sentence.
- Adequate development of a paragraph means that the main idea is supported with sufficient detail and explanation so that the reader understands exactly what you mean.

Exercise 1-1:   Distinguishing general and specific statements

DIRECTIONS: *In each pair of statements, one statement is general and the other is specific. On the line at the left, write* **G** *for the general statement and* **S** *for the specific.*

Example: __G__   a. School closed because of bad weather.

　　　　　__S__   b. When the temperature hit −20 degrees and the snowfall measured 10 inches, school was closed for the day.

_____ 1. a. Though my flight was scheduled to arrive at 5:10 P.M., it did not arrive until 6:20 P.M.

_____ 1. b. My plane was delayed in taking off from Atlanta, so it arrived here an hour or so late.

_____ 2. a. The starting pitcher on our home team has set an outstanding record for several consecutive years.

_____ 2. b. Roger Twain won the Cy Young award for three consecutive years.

_____ 3. a. The officer believed that she was dealing with a drunk driver.

_____ 3. b. The officer saw that the driver's face was red, and his eyes were bloodshot; when asked to walk a straight line, the driver staggered and almost fell down.

_____ 4. a. Jumping out of a plane is so exciting that it causes physical reactions for the skydiver.

_____ 4. b. Jumping out of a plane makes the blood rush to the head and pushes the air out of the lungs.

_____ 5. a. The police officer arrested the robbery suspect after she had investigated for six days and spent three tense hours waiting in front of the suspect's house.

_____ 5. b. Police work requires patience and persistence.

_____ 6. a. My cousin is such an accomplished chef that she can make even fish stew taste good.

_____ 6. b. My cousin, who runs the kitchen at a four-star restaurant, won last year's Premier Dining Award for her outstanding bouillabaisse.

_____ 7. a. The word *kiwi* refers to a vine that bears a fuzzy, edible fruit and to flightless birds of New Zealand.

_____ 7. b. The word *kiwi* has two meanings, completely unrelated to each other.

_____ 8. a. Fad diets can be a threat to our pocketbooks.

_____ 8. b. Each year Americans spend about $74 million on fad diets.

_____ 9. a. Hernando Cortès was a European explorer who lived many years ago.

_____ 9. b. Hernando Cortès was a Spanish explorer who lived from 1485 to 1547.

_____ 10. a. Centipedes and millipedes, insects with many pairs of feet, have names derived from the root "ped," meaning foot.

_____ 10. b. Like other living creatures, some insects are named for distinctive features of their bodies.

Exercise 1-2:   Making general statements more specific

DIRECTIONS: *The statements below are general. Improve them by follow-ing these steps:*

   1. Underline the part of the statement that is too general.

   2. Write a revised statement, using the same ideas but giving specific in-formation.

Example: We spent our vacation in <u>a large national park.</u>

We vacationed for ten days at Mammoth Cave National Park, a beautiful reservation of seventy-nine square miles in central Kentucky.

1. I saw a good movie last Saturday.

   _____

   _____

   _____

2. My car gives me a lot of trouble.

   _____

   _____

   _____

3. That man over there is an excellent pitcher to have on the team.

   _____

   _____

   _____

4. One turning point in my life was really dramatic.

   _____

   _____

   _____

5. Trees can grow very tall if they are allowed to live long enough.

_____

_____

_____

6. Monica is a talented artist.

_____

_____

_____

7. I had a lot of anxiety about starting college.

_____

_____

_____

8. Cars cost much more now than they ever did before.

_____

_____

_____

9. Computer literacy can be important, even for entry-level jobs.

_____

_____

_____

10. The state park is crowded on holiday weekends.

_____

_____

_____

Exercise 1-3:   Creating specific supporting ideas

DIRECTIONS: *List three specific ideas that come to mind about these general ideas.*

Example: Attending a rock concert

    a. The struggle to get tickets for good seats
    b. Bizarre clothing worn by the musicians or members of the audience
    c. Comparisons between hearing music live and hearing recordings

1. Applying for a job

    a. _____

    b. _____

    c. _____

2. Entering military service

    a. _____

    b. _____

    c. _____

3. Getting settled into a new home

    a. _____

    b. _____

    c. _____

4. Planning a vacation

    a. _____

    b. _____

    c. _____

5. Facing death or bereavement

    a. _____

b. _____

c. _____

6. Early childhood memories

a. _____

b. _____

c. _____

7. A family heirloom or family tradition

a. _____

b. _____

c. _____

8. A big disappointment

a. _____

b. _____

c. _____

9. My first day on a new job

a. _____

b. _____

c. _____

10. An important issue in my community or apartment complex

a. _____

b. _____

c. _____

Exercise 1-4:   Looking at drafts

DIRECTIONS: *The examples below are drafts written by students at the beginning of a term. They wrote in class for about an hour, using any one of these topics:*

1. *An object that has special meaning for me*

2. *A favorite pastime or hobby*

3. *An accomplishment that makes me proud*

As you read these paragraphs, draw a line through irrelevant statements. In the margins, write "too general" or "good specific detail" or any other comments that apply. Compare your impressions with those of your classmates.

#1:

[1]Romance novels give me relaxation and show me ways of handling problems. [2]I work thirty hours a week and take two college courses, so I don't have much time to read for fun. [3]But when I do, I like romances. [4]My husband likes mystery novels, but he doesn't have much time to read either. [5]He works full time in town, then helps his folks on their farm most weekends. [6]Romances take me away from pressure for an hour or so a week. [7]I don't like pressure, and it sure doesn't like me. [8]I like to imagine myself in the exciting situations of the characters. [9]A lot of times they are rich and have fancy clothes and cars. [10]The characters don't lead perfect lives, and they always have problems. [11]When they do have troubles, I think about how I would solve those problems. [12]Then I compare what I would do with what they do. [13]Usually my husband and I talk things out and settle our differences. [14]Sometimes the characters in romances take the long way around their problems. [15]They make matters worse by lying and covering up. [16]It would be so much easier for them if they would handle their problems as my husband and I do. [17]We just talk and settle our differences.

#2:

[1]I have a unicorn necklace that means a lot to me. [2]My necklace has a crystal stone in it. [3]It is a unicorn with a flowing mane and a crystal in the horn. [4]The unicorn and chain are made of sterling silver that gives it an antique look and feel. [5]I got my unicorn when I quit drinking. [6]I got it because it helped me celebrate my new life, and it was on sale. [7]To me

the unicorn is a higher power that has helped me quit drinking, stop smoking, go back to school, and just generally feel better about myself. [8]When I get discouraged, I hold my necklace, and it reminds me to keep my chin up and keep trying. [9]Otherwise, I feel so blue, I don't know what to do; it's true, because it helps me with the things that I do. [10]The necklace seems to give me power over my life. [11]I know that I could live without the necklace, but I don't believe I could conquer life's potholes as easily or confidently. [12]My boyfriend has a crystal also, but I don't think it gives him the power I feel, because he started smoking again. [13]He smells like a furnace because of it, but I love him anyway.

#3:

[1]I am proud that I overcame my fear of heights and learned to pilot a plane myself. [2]I have felt proud of many achievements in my life, but my solo flight stands out most. [3]It was not only a matter of learning the controls or understanding the principles of flight. [4]For me, being a pilot also meant that I had to overcome lifelong uneasiness about heights. [5]Looking back on the experience now, I feel that the months of preparation and training went by quickly. [6]They are now a blur in my mind. [7]But I will always remember my fears as I taxied down the field toward the runway before taking off alone. [8]I couldn't help wondering what I would do if things went wrong. [9]I kept asking myself if I would forget to do something important. [10]When I lifted off the ground, however, my doubts disappeared, and I felt the power of the plane and pride in my achievement.

Exercise 1-5:   Creating a draft

DIRECTIONS: *On separate paper, write on one of the topics in Exercise 1-2, 1-3, or 1-4 above, or use topics suggested by your teacher.*

Spend about an hour, writing steadily. Try to stick to your topic and be specific. Divide the material into more than one paragraph if you like.

Exercise 1-6:   Examining students' paragraphs in peer groups

DIRECTIONS: *Revise the draft created in Exercise 1-5. As you work, consider each of the questions below. Use the guidelines in Appendix A as you prepare your final copy.*

Bring three copies of your paragraph to class. Work in a small group with your classmates. They will read your paragraph, and you will read theirs. Find the good features in these paragraphs. Then discuss how the paragraphs can be improved. As you read and discuss them, keep these points in mind:

1. What is the main point of the paragraph?

2. Which is the topic sentence?

3. Are the supporting sentences specific enough, or are they too general? Point out which ones need to be more specific.

4. Overall, has the writer provided enough specific information to support the main idea well?

5. What else might readers want or need to know about this topic?

6. Does the paragraph have unity? Are all the supporting ideas relevant, or has the writer strayed away from the main idea?

7. Do you sense order in what the student has written? For instance, if the writer is presenting ideas chronologically, is the time sequence clear to you? Or if the writer is moving from the least important to the most important statements, is that progression clear?

8. Do the sentences flow smoothly from one to another? Do the ideas seem to lead naturally from one to another?

2

Finding Topics

Your first step in writing is finding a topic. Sometimes you have no choice: you must write on a specified topic, or you must choose one of a few suggested topics. But at other times you are free to write on any topic you like, or you can narrow and shape a general topic as you like.

No matter how much freedom you have, first think about your audience—that is, your readers. Consider your purpose in writing to those readers. With these two considerations in mind, think about your interests and background. Then you will be able to discover and develop a topic for writing.

Considering Audience and Purpose

The young man looked troubled as he walked into his teacher's office. He was carrying his latest paper. The teacher knew that this student struggled with writing and worried a lot about his grades. She also knew that he had taken special interest in this last paper, and it showed. "Todd, this is the best writing you have done so far," she said, wondering why he had come to see her.

After Todd sat down, they talked for a few minutes until he got to his point. Then, hesitantly, with eyes cast down, he almost whispered his question: "Do you think I might fix up this paper and submit it to *Reader's Digest* or somewhere? Maybe it would help someone else to know what I went through."

Todd had discovered what writing is all about, though he might not have been aware of it just then. Writing is not about pleasing teachers, getting grades, or satisfying college requirements. It is not about typing neat papers, checking spelling, or following grammar rules. These details do matter, but writing is truly what Todd had in mind: sharing our experiences and thoughts with others.

Todd had written about his father's death and its effect on the family, but particularly on Todd himself. He began by describing his father's long illness, the family's sense of helplessness, and his own anguish. Just before his father died, the family had gathered at the hospital, and each person spent a few minutes with him privately. When writing his paper, Todd had gone over those last moments in his mind.

As Todd and his teacher talked, they agreed that writing has been a healing step in his grieving. Such an idea is far from novel: throughout history, men and women have written to sort out their thoughts and feelings. At times there is no substitute for writing to ease one's feelings.

Practice 2-1. Thinking about private uses for writing

DIRECTIONS: *Have you ever wanted to get away from the stresses of life and just write to yourself about something? What was the occasion? Mention such a time that you are willing to share with others.*

_____

_____

Beyond writing to serve our private needs, we often need to share our thoughts and feelings with others—that is, to communicate. Todd was typical in wanting to help others deal with loss and bereavement. It is not just professional writers who want to communicate; anyone who has a purpose for writing and readers in mind can communicate.

Readers make up a group called an "audience," meaning receivers of messages. The word "audience" suggests that writing is usually a public performance that others will see or hear. The word also implies that readers may act like audiences elsewhere. They may approve or disapprove, agree or disagree, but they are likely to be interested and attentive.

Good writers help readers understand their messages. They provide explanations and definitions to help the audience. They organize so that main points stand out. In short, good writers want to communicate with others, but they realize that wanting is not enough. They know that writing well requires planning and careful attention to details, but that communicating with readers makes the effort worthwhile.

After talking to his teacher, Todd worked on his paper again. He revised to make each statement as clear as possible to readers. He reconsidered the order of his ideas, his wording, and in short, every feature of his paper. His teacher did not see the final version, nor did she find out whether he actually submitted his story to a magazine. But at that moment Todd knew the meaning of writing with an audience and a purpose in mind.

Practice 2-2. Thinking about sharing ideas in writing

DIRECTIONS: *Have you ever wanted to write to a friend, eager to share something? Mention an occasion that you are willing to let others know about.*

What was written? _____

_____

Who was the audience? _____

_____

Did you get a response? _____

If you got a response, think about it again. Judging by that response, did

your reader understand what you were feeling at that moment? _____

_____

_____

Many people write privately, just to please or comfort themselves at times. Most people also write to share thoughts and experiences with others. Almost everyone also writes for impersonal, practical reasons. At school and at work, writing is demanded, whether we like it or not, whether we feel like it or not, whether we are inspired to do it or not.

Practice 2-3.   Thinking about writing at work

DIRECTIONS: *Consider the job you have now or the job you want to have five years from now. What kinds of writing does that job require? Consider such possibilities as reports, responses to letters, memos to supervisors and coworkers, advertising copy, and proposals.*

Type of job

_____

Occasions for writing

1. _____

2. _____

On the job, employees usually have specific purposes for writing and specific readers in mind. They may write to customers, solving problems or answering questions. They may write guidelines for new employees and proposals for new projects. They may prepare advertising copy or reports for stockholders. Many jobs involve these and other situations that demand writing.

Practice 2-4.   Thinking about readers of work-related writing

DIRECTIONS: *Look at your responses in Practice 2-3. Who will read your writing? List three possible members of your audience:*

1. _____

2. _____

3. _____

Whether you are writing on the job or elsewhere, you will sometimes know your readers personally, but often you will not. If you are writing a memo to your coworkers, you know at least some of them personally, depending upon the size of the company. But if you are writing a letter to your representative in the state legislature or in Congress, you may not know that person except by reputation.

As you think about your readers, you are also thinking about your reasons for writing to them. Audience and purpose are connected. You may be writing to achieve one of these purposes:

- inform
- explain
- persuade
- entertain
- offer help
- ask for something
- answer questions

These and many other reasons may prompt your writing. The purposes vary greatly, but your writing *does* have a purpose.

Different readers have very different interests and need different kinds of information. As much as possible, anticipate your readers' needs and direct your writing along those lines.

Practice 2-5.   Considering different readers' needs

DIRECTIONS: *A large department store is planning its annual clearance sale. Various people need various kinds of information about this event, including the kinds of information listed below. Add other bits of information needed by these "audiences":*

1. Customers

   when the sale begins

   a. _____

   b. _____

2. Sales staff

   how to enter sale prices into computer terminals

   a. _____

   b. _____

3. Advertising-department staff

   which sale items to feature in newspaper ads

a. _____

b. _____

Besides giving your readers the information they need, you will sometimes write to convince others of a point of view. You may want to persuade readers about social, political, religious, or community issues. At other times, you may want to persuade them on matters of health or safety. You might have an original message, or you might use a common message such as "Don't drink and drive." Whenever you have a message to convey and you are not sure how to approach the topic, begin by asking yourself questions like these:

- What do I know that provides evidence for this position?
- What can I suggest as a solution or alternative?
- Who could give me information?
- How much information can I find in libraries?

Practice 2-6.   Finding information

DIRECTIONS: *Select one of these messages. Where would you look for information about that message? List three possible sources.*

a. *We must recycle newspapers in our community.*
b. *Contrary to popular opinion, some houses are truly haunted.*
c. *Don't drink and drive.*
d. *Leasing a car actually costs less than buying.*
e. *The AIDS epidemic is a threat to every American.*

1. _____

2. _____

3. _____

Sometimes audience and purpose are fairly obvious. At other times, as in Todd's situation, the purpose is clear, but the audience is not. Todd wanted to share, but with whom? He thought of readers of a magazine as a possibility. The important thing is that he felt he needed an audience, a necessity that too often is overlooked entirely.

As a student, you have more freedom in choosing topics for writing than do workers on the job. You may feel a lack of purpose and audience, though, except for the obvious: you must finish assignments and work for grades, and your teacher is an audience.

Unfortunately, in school it is easy to forget audiences and purposes beyond the classroom. It is also easy to forget that writing means communicating with many varied audiences for many reasons. Audience and purpose are stressed here because they will be vital to your writing, not just in school, but throughout your life.

Brainstorming and Prewriting

Perhaps you have thought something like this: "I can't write because I have nothing to write about. Nothing interesting ever happens to me." If you feel that way, remember that no one else can ever be exactly like you. You are unique, and so your experiences and your views about them are unique. This part of the chapter suggests ways by which you can bring out some of your memories, reactions, beliefs, and impressions—all as possible topics for writing. Then you can select some of those to share with your audience.

As a start, think about your experience in writing. Recall which techniques worked for you, including a setting in which you have felt comfortable when writing. If possible, get into that comfortable setting.

Then think of a topic and let your mind wander. Jot down all the related ideas you can think of within a few minutes. You will be **brainstorming,** that is, letting your ideas flow without regard for order or relevance. Just keep pouring out ideas. Later you can sort, discard (if necessary), and refine those ideas.

Practice 2-7.　Recalling experience and brainstorming

DIRECTIONS:　*What setting works best for you when writing? Do you need a quiet room, or do you like music playing in the background? Can you write more easily at some times of the day?*

_____

_____

_____

If you compare your responses with those of your classmates, you will find a wide range of reactions, none of which are right or wrong: whatever works well for you is right for you.

Now, for a few minutes, brainstorm on this topic:

The perfect setting in which I could relax and write

_____

_____

_____

_____

_____

Brainstorming is not a final goal. Rather, it is a useful method for generating ideas to write about. Many people find brainstorming helpful **after** they think of a general topic to use as a starting point. Then brainstorming often leads to a more specific topic for writing, or it may generate supporting material for the original topic. Occasionally brainstorming leads to a completely different topic. Whatever the results, brainstorming is a device worth trying.

But first, you must find a starting point, a general topic about which to brainstorm. The ideal topic is one that genuinely interests you. Then you will have a topic about which you know something already, and about which you enjoy thinking. Writing will seem easier because your interest pushes you along and you will probably also communicate your enthusiasm for that topic. Attitudes do come through in writing, so that you are better off with topics about which you have strong, positive feelings.

If a general topic is assigned and it does not interest you, try to find some appealing angle and work with that. You can use your background and interests in narrowing big, general topics to manageable, specific topics.

Suppose you are taking a course in American history, and you must write a paper on the Civil War period. Your teacher wants you to choose a historic figure or a battle to focus on. At first you dread the assignment, feeling that the topic is boring, but then you recall that you visited Vicksburg, Mississippi. Because of that experience you may be drawn toward events at Vicksburg. Perhaps you can write about General Ulysses S. Grant or General John C. Pemberton in the battle of Vicksburg. Because of your visit, you can envision the city's geography and imagine the positions held by the troops on both sides.

All of us have more resources than we realize, in the form of memories and experiences we can draw upon. A sample of those resources is shown in Practice 2-8. Making your additions, you will create a personal list.

Practice 2-8. Finding possible topics for writing

DIRECTIONS: *Add two possible topics in each of the categories below, drawing upon your own experience and background.*

1. *Memories of people*

   my grandfather's love of fishing

   a. _____

   b. _____

2. *Memories of times and places*

   an early morning, during autumn, first day of duck hunting

   a. _____

   b. _____

3. *Memories of events*

   my parents' silver wedding anniversary

   a. _____

   b. _____

4. *Memories of happy experiences*

   making the winning touchdown during a big game

   a. _____

   b. _____

5. *Memories of unhappy experiences*

   being pulled over by a police officer

   a. _____

   b. _____

6. *Strong feelings*

   anger over a divorce in the family

a. _____

b. _____

After you find a possible topic, brainstorming helps you generate supporting ideas. By listing ideas as they come to mind, you discover the raw materials from which a paragraph or longer piece of writing can be built. The list gets you started thinking. Then, while you write, you will think of still other ideas.

Here is an example of one student's brainstorming and prewriting:

Starting point: Music is an important part of my life

List generated by brainstorming:
  began playing the flute in fifth grade
  music still my favorite hobby
  learned a lot because of music
  work out anger, frustrations with music
  play the flute or piano when angry
  learned discipline by practice
  parents forced me to practice at first
  learned breath control
  never helped with singing, never could sing
  played in band concerts all through school
  learned to be confident playing in public
  got to play a solo in senior-year spring concert
  still enjoy flute and piano
  music made me confident
  had to overcome stage fright
  music made me a better person

This list is a typical start for a large, rather vague topic; it covers lots of territory, showing that the student had many experiences to draw upon. Most of the items are too big and general, but they could be narrowed down with specific details.

But first—before adding, dropping, or changing any of the items— this student looked at her list again. She could see that brainstorming had generated some items that are more important than others. To see more clearly what she had, she grouped related ideas, like this:

1. How music has fit into my life
      began playing the flute in fifth grade
      music still my favorite hobby
      still enjoy flute and piano

2. How music helps me
   work out anger, frustrations with music
   play the flute or piano when angry
3. What I have learned through music
   learned discipline by practice
   learned breath control
   learned to be confident playing in public

General statements must be supported with specific information, as shown in Chapter 1. Within the third grouping, some ideas are more specific than others and they do support larger concepts. For instance, this is a large concept:

learned breath control

Set off by breath control, the writer immediately thought of singing, and during brainstorming she added this detail:

never helped with singing, never could sing

But singing is off the track. The paragraph is about this writer's experiences. Obviously she plays the flute and the piano. Those instruments are mentioned several times, but singing is mentioned only this once. The logical next step is to throw away this item and support "learned breath control" with a relevant detail.

Practice 2-9. Creating specific statements

DIRECTIONS: *Suggest details that would support these statements.*

General: I learned breath control by playing the flute.

Specific: _____

_____

General: I played in band concerts all through school.

Specific: _____

_____

General: I learned to be confident playing in public.

Specific: _____

_____

This student had many ideas to share about her experiences with music. By brainstorming she generated a list of possible items. Grouping the items revealed a part of the topic that she could write about. It also showed that some of the items generated by brainstorming had to be discarded.

The student's experience is typical. Writers often begin with overly large, general topics. Brainstorming and grouping items can lead to a more exact, smaller portion of that general topic. Then specific supporting ideas can be developed.

In Chapter 3, we discuss the next step toward writing a clear, focused paragraph. That step is forming a strong, well-worded topic sentence. Sometimes you will think of your topic idea while you brainstorm, group, and refine general ideas into more specific ones. At other times, you will develop the topic idea later in your writing. But your starting point is always finding a workable topic and generating relevant ideas about that topic.

Summary

- The purpose of writing is communication—that is, sharing our thoughts and feelings with others.

- Writing serves as a means of personal discovery and as a means for communicating with others.

- Writing serves practical purposes in our daily lives in school and on the job. The purpose and audience may be evident.

- When possible, write about topics that interest you. If that is not possible, look for interesting points within the assigned topic.

- Because your attitudes show through your writing, try to select topics that will bring out strong, positive feelings.

- Brainstorming is a device for generating ideas on a topic. Let each idea lead to another without stopping to consider their order or relevance.

- After brainstorming, sort and group ideas. Throw away irrelevant ideas and revise overly general ones.

- Before writing, replace general statements with more specific ones.

Exercise 2-1:   Generating topics for writing

DIRECTIONS: *The questions below will bring to mind topics you could write about. List topics as responses to these questions. One topic has been suggested for each question.*

1. What have you read that is memorable?

   a. Graffiti on a wall, one of them saying "Thou shalt not doodle."

   b. _____

   _____

   c. _____

   _____

   d. _____

   _____

2. What have you seen that was vivid or unusual?

   a. An airplane landing on a highway.

   b. _____

   _____

   c. _____

   _____

   d. _____

   _____

3. What have you heard that is important to you in some way?

   a. The second test proved that my friend did not have AIDS.

   b. _____

   _____

c. _____

_____

d. _____

_____

4. What have you felt in an unusual situation?

a. I was terrified while riding on that steep, winding mountain road because the dropoff beside the roadway was a sheer cliff, thousands of feet down.

b. _____

_____

c. _____

_____

d. _____

_____

5. What did you see on campus recently that you did not expect to see?

a. So many older people coming to classes. It's great!

b. _____

_____

c. _____

_____

d. _____

_____

6. If you could spend fifteen minutes with the President of the United States, what positions would you encourage him to take on the issues of the day?

a. I would urge the President to budget more money for medical research, especially for cancer and AIDS.

b. _____

_____

_____

c. _____

_____

_____

d. _____

_____

_____

7. What changes are needed in your workplace to make it safer, pleasanter, or more convenient?

a. This company needs better patrols and security for the parking areas, particularly better lighting at night.

b. _____

_____

_____

c. _____

_____

_____

d. _____

_____

_____

Exercise 2-2:   Narrowing topics

DIRECTIONS: *List specific topics that might be used by a writer dealing with these general topics.*

Example: Dealing with drug problems in a neighborhood

   a. Trying to ensure safety for residents
   b. Finding proper treatment for cocaine babies
   c. Working to apprehend dealers

1. Adapting to life in a new country or community

   a. _____

   b. _____

   c. _____

2. Dealing with a serious illness or injury

   a. _____

   b. _____

   c. _____

3. Overcoming racial prejudice

   a. _____

   b. _____

   c. _____

4. Planning a wedding

   a. _____

   b. _____

   c. _____

5. Helping children form religious beliefs

   a. _____

   b. _____

   c. _____

6. Ways to lose or gain weight (one or the other)

   a. _____

   b. _____

   c. _____

7. Clothes I would buy if I could afford them

   a. _____

   b. _____

   c. _____

8. This season's best television shows

   a. _____

   b. _____

   c. _____

9. Ways of raising money for a worthy community project

   a. _____

   b. _____

   c. _____

10. Reasons I am attending college

   a. _____

   b. _____

   c. _____

Exercise 2-3:   Grouping ideas generated by brainstorming

DIRECTIONS: *The topics given below were used by students for writing paragraphs. The ideas listed in each group were used in those students' paragraphs.*

Examine each group carefully and put a line through any idea that seems irrelevant or off the track.

Then rearrange the rest of the ideas into groups. Write in the right margin, as shown in the example.

Example

Topic: my grandpa's love of fishing

Grandpa lives on a farm.
The farm has a pond.
Most years the pond is full.
A small creek flows into the pond.
The pond usually has lots of fish.
Those fish are not worth eating.
Grandma hates cleaning fish.
Uncle Ned goes fishing at a state park.
Dad never liked to fish.
I learned to fish from Grandpa.
He had patience, unlike Uncle Ned.
The creek ran dry last year.
The pond was low and poor for fishing.

pond—
full of water
many fish,
not all edible
water low last year

other relatives—
Uncle Ned
Dad
Grandma

Problem 1

Topic: playing hockey

I started at age four.
I picked up skill quickly.
My older brothers helped me.
I played in the Mite League.
The league is for beginners.
I spent lots of time.
I saw many coaching styles.
After school I shot pucks in the basement.
I had to develop skill in skating.
I went to summer hockey school.

I am proud of my achievements.

In high school I made the top varsity team.

Our team was very competitive.

I practiced from grade school on.

Starting early was good for me.

Playing well really takes dedication.

Problem 2

Topic: attending professional modeling school

I went last summer on my day off.

It was hard because I had just one day off.

The course included classes on makeup, posture, and wardrobe.

I made a scrapbook of ideas during the course.

We had photographic sessions twice.

We could work for awards in the course. I wanted to win for the best scrapbook.

We practiced for a final fashion show.

I wanted to win the award for the show also.

We had five months to work on the scrapbook.

The runway show was at graduation.

I won the trophy for that show.

It was a thrilling moment.

Then my scrapbook won an award.

The scrapbook was due the day of graduation.

The graduation performance went well.

Problem 3

Topic: finding my birth mother

I'm lucky to have two mothers.

I am adopted.

I don't remember when my parents told me I'm adopted.

My parents are wonderful to me.

I was always curious about my real mother.

Why did she give me up for adoption?

What does she look like?

Is she even alive now?

Last year I got the answers.

For thirty years, she had a lot of questions in her mind, too.

She had been looking for me.

We met and got acquainted.

Now I have two mothers who love me.

I am very lucky.

I want to spend more time with my birth mother.

My family is understanding and respects my feelings.

I do not want to hurt my family.

Exercise 2-4:   Brainstorming and grouping ideas

DIRECTIONS: *Select any three of the topics below, any of the topics men-*
tioned in Exercise 2-2, or any topic of your choice. For each of the topics you
select, list ten or more items that come to mind at once.
   Write on separate paper.
   If it helps you to generate ideas, brainstorm with one or more classmates.
   After you have three lists of items, revise and group the items according
to some logical arrangement. Compare your lists with those of others in
your class.

Example

   Sample topic: This year's all-star baseball game

Brainstorming items

hard to get tickets
two local players made the team
no local players on last year's team
tickets very expensive
may have to work that night anyway
getting time off may not be possible
last year's game was a bore
last year's game too one-sided (9–2)
taking time off from work costs me money
went last year with my girlfriend
have a different girlfriend now

Grouping of items

1. Problems with getting tickets
    hard to get tickets
    tickets very expensive

2. Conflicts with work schedule
    may have to work that night anyway
    getting time off may not be possible
    taking time off from work costs me money

3. Disappointment with last year's game
    last year's game was a bore
    last year's game too one-sided(9–2)

4. Differences between last year and this year
    went last year with my girlfriend
    have a different girlfriend now
    two local players made the team
    no local players on last year's team

Possible topics

1. Airport noise or low-flying aircraft or both
2. High-school proms
3. A recruiting officer's promises
4. New cars in a dealer's showroom
5. Pollution in a local river or lake
6. Devices used by junk-mail advertisers
7. Pros or cons of telephone answering machines
8. A phobia (select any you care about)
9. Political cartoons
10. Parking regulations on campus
11. Bad advice I heard as a youngster
12. Unusual clothing styles on campus (or elsewhere)
13. Antique cars
14. Problems in learning a second language
15. Foods that I had to learn to like

Exercise 2-5: Brainstorming on a topic of your choice

DIRECTIONS: *Remember Todd, whose experience was described at the opening of this chapter. Select a topic that matters to you as his topic mattered to him. You may use a response you wrote in any exercise above, provided one of those topics genuinely matters to you.*

Consider sharing your ideas with an audience beyond the classroom. For instance, you might write to let your friends in high school know what to expect in college.

Use brainstorming to generate some supporting ideas. Then group the ideas as shown in Exercises 2-3 and 2-4. Eliminate the ones that are irrelevant, and refine the overly general statements into more specific statements.

Unlike Exercise 2-4 in which you worked with others, this exercise should be done alone. Write on separate paper.

Exercise 2-6: Writing a paragraph on a topic of your choice

DIRECTIONS: *Write a paragraph on the ideas you generated in Exercise 2-5. If your teacher so directs, turn in Exercise 2-5 with your paragraph.*

3

Writing Topic Sentences

Understanding the Topic Sentence

The topic sentence states the main idea of a paragraph. For that reason it is the most important sentence in the paragraph. Writers build paragraphs to support topic sentences, and readers rely on these sentences to see which main ideas are being developed.

The topic sentence does two things:

1. It announces the general topic of the paragraph. The topic sentence is often at the beginning of the paragraph, but it can be elsewhere within the paragraph. The general topic of the paragraph is usually the subject of the topic sentence.
2. It limits the paragraph to some specific, manageable part of the general topic. This limited part of the general topic is often called the **controlling idea.** Often the latter part of the topic sentence (the part that includes the verb or follows the verb) limits the scope of the paragraph. That part of the sentence expresses the controlling idea.

Consider these topic sentences:

a. The main benefit in being a paper carrier was that I learned to take responsibility.
b. The main benefit in being a bartender is that I meet many interesting and unusual people.
c. The main benefit in being a nurse in a children's hospital is the satisfaction of helping the sick children.

d. The main benefit in being a sales representative is my sense of independence.

These four topic sentences start a lot alike because they all announce the same general topic, namely, the main benefit in doing a job. The paragraphs using these topic sentences would deal with the subjects of the sentences: the main benefit in being a paper carrier, a bartender, a nurse, or a sales representative.

But those four topic sentences are also very different because they limit the paragraphs to four different, specific benefits. In each of these sentences the latter part holds the controlling idea. That idea states exactly which specific benefit the paragraph will cover.

Here are the same topic sentences with the controlling ideas underlined:

a. The main benefit in being a paper carrier was that <u>I learned to take responsibility.</u>
b. The main benefit in being a bartender is that <u>I meet many interesting and unusual people.</u>
c. The main benefit in being a nurse in a children's hospital is <u>the satisfaction of helping the sick children.</u>
d. The main benefit in being a sales representative is <u>my sense of independence.</u>

Paragraphs using sample topic sentences a, b, c, and d would be limited to the underlined controlling ideas. Thus, one paragraph would explain how carrying papers taught the writer to take responsibility. In that paragraph, all the sentences would have to pertain to that leading idea. In another paragraph the writer would explain "interesting and unusual people" and probably give examples. In that paragraph, all the sentences would have to pertain to those interesting and unusual people.

It helps to think of the topic sentence as a writer's promise to the reader. The writer promises to discuss a specified main idea. Suppose the topic sentence is item d above:

The main benefit in being a sales representative is <u>my sense of independence.</u>

By writing that topic sentence, the writer promises to discuss the sense of independence that comes from being a sales representative. If the writer discussed commissions, sales meetings, or selling strategies instead of that "sense of independence," the promise would be broken.

As a writer, you are responsible for shaping your topic sentences so that they express exactly what you want to say. Then, as you write, you are expected to stick to the controlling ideas in your topic sentences.

Practice 3-1. Identifying topics and controlling ideas

DIRECTIONS: *In these topic sentences, circle the general topics and underline the controlling ideas.*

1. Registration for my first term in college was very time-consuming because I had to wait in long lines.

2. Registration for my first term in college was frustrating because two of the classes I wanted to take were closed.

3. Registration for my first term in college went so smoothly that I was amazed.

4. Starting college at age thirty-seven made me uneasy until I met other older students.

5. Enrolling in a business curriculum is a natural choice because of my fifteen years of business experience.

6. Finding study time is hard because of my work and family obligations.

When you begin to think about a topic, you are starting to consider the main point that you might make. At first, you may not realize how many main points you could discuss. Then, as you brainstorm, group ideas, and begin to write, many possibilities come to mind. Eventually you will settle on one of them.

Suppose you want to write about your experience when registering for classes. The first memory that comes to mind is standing in long lines. But as you think about that day again, you realize that the long lines were not very important. What really mattered was that some classes you wanted to take were already closed. As you think about that fact, you recall your frustration. Your paragraph might ultimately be based on this topic sentence:

Registration for this term was frustrating because two classes I wanted to take were already closed.

After you select the main idea you want to discuss in your paragraph, you can shape the topic sentence accordingly. That sentence will express the general idea and a controlling idea. It will convey your main point to the reader.

Developing Clarity and Exactness

You must select a main idea that you **can** discuss in a paragraph, and a main idea that you **want** to discuss. As you consider possible topic ideas, it will help to keep these guidelines in mind:

- A good topic sentence states an idea that requires explanation. With informative writing you may state a fact, then elaborate upon it. For example:

  Acceptable: The Bill of Rights establishes ten basic freedoms.

                 or

                 Installing the vent requires four steps.

  If the topic sentence states a fact, it should not be an obvious fact that requires no explanation. Instead, it should be a fact that needs explanation.

  Too obvious: The Rocky Mountain states are in the western United States.

                  or

                  Denver is a large city in Colorado.

  The topic sentence is more likely to express an attitude about a fact, and it does so in fairly specific words.

  Poor: The Rocky Mountain states are nice places to live.
  Better: The Rocky Mountain states are among the most livable in the United States.

- A good topic sentence states an idea that is narrow enough to be discussed in one paragraph.

  Poor: The Rocky Mountain states are among the most livable in the United States.
  Better: Living in Colorado Springs, Colorado, is very pleasant because of the beautiful environment.

- A good topic sentence makes an exact statement, not a vague one.

  Poor: Living in Colorado Springs, Colorado, is very pleasant because of the beautiful environment.
  Better: Living in Colorado Springs, Colorado, gives me the opportunity to enjoy Pike's Peak and the Garden of the Gods.

Practice 3-2.   Narrowing topic ideas

DIRECTIONS: *Revise these topic ideas to narrow their scope and to make them more exact.*

Example: Some music can bring back memories from my high school years.

Revision: Whenever I hear Amy Grant songs, I am reminded of the hours our gymnastic team worked out while listening to her music.

1. My daughter seemed to be happy with her birthday gifts.

_____

_____

_____

2. Being a single parent is very difficult.

_____

_____

_____

3. It is hard to get by on the minimum hourly wage.

_____

_____

_____

4. My job has a lot of monotonous repetition.

_____

_____

_____

5. A lot of situations in life can make people unhappy.

_____

_____

_____

As you draft your paragraphs, you will often begin with general topic ideas, similar to the five statements in Practice 3-2. You must revise those ideas because they are too large to be discussed in one paragraph. Narrow those large topics into smaller, more manageable subjects, just as you did in revising the five statements in Practice 3-2.

After you narrow the topic idea, you are ready to shape the topic sentence itself. Then, while you work on that sentence, keep these tips in mind:

- Be sure you are expressing your topic idea in a complete thought, not a fragment. A topic sentence is a full sentence. It is not to be confused with a title.

  Poor: The most difficult problem faced by a single parent. (This is a sentence fragment.)
             or
             A Single Parent's Most Difficult Problem (This is a title.)
  Better: The most difficult problem faced by a single parent is supporting the family.
             or
             The most difficult problem a single parent faces is finding enough time to spend with each of the children.

- Use a sentence that expresses one clear, dominant idea, not two or more equally important ideas.

  Poor: I am proud of being an accomplished softball player, and I worked very hard to develop the skill.
  Better: Though it was hard for me to acquire my skill, I am proud of being an accomplished softball player. (Here the emphasis is on being an accomplished softball player.)
             or
             Though I am proud of being an accomplished softball player, I am even prouder of the hard work I put into developing my skill. (Here the emphasis is on the hard work I put into developing my skill.)

> *Poor:*   The college allows only three weeks for registration, but five weeks would be better, considering how many students need to register.
>
> *Better:*   Extending registration from the present three weeks to five would make the procedure easier for students.

- Use statements rather than questions. Topic sentences should express the writer's ideas, not throw questions at readers.

    Poor: Who wouldn't be frustrated with the long lines at registration?

    Better: With better planning, the college could eliminate the congestion and long lines during registration.

    Poor: Why should anyone give up a good job to go back to school?

    Better: Though I had a good job, I returned to school to learn new skills that will help me advance.

- Express yourself in your own words, not in stale, commonplace clichés. If your topic is familiar to readers, try to stimulate interest by expressing an original point of view.

    Stale: My supervisor's bark is worse than her bite.

    Clear: Though my supervisor seems gruff at times, she is really fair and reasonable.

    Commonplace: American high school students should get a good background in math.

    Better: High school students should be free to take as much or as little math as they want.

    or

    All high school students should be required to take math every year.

Practice 3-3.   Revising topic sentences

DIRECTIONS: *Improve these sentences, using the guidelines above.*

Example: I started college after being out of school for twelve years, and it was a big adjustment.

Revision: When I began college after twelve years away from school, I had to adjust to studying again.

1. Why is betting on ball games a bad practice?

_____

_____

_____

2. One of my uncles was a habitual gambler, and eventually he lost his home and business.

_____

_____

_____

3. The frightening experience of being mistaken for someone else.

_____

_____

_____

4. Taking part in speech and drama is a useful experience.

_____

_____

_____

5. Consumers can save a lot of money if they buy clothing during clearance sales.

_____

_____

_____

Writing your own topic sentences is sure to be more interesting than revising someone else's poor ones, such as those in the practice section above. You may have to move through many steps to create good topic sentences. Many times the writing is time-consuming, but it is well worth the effort because a good topic sentence is essential for a strong paragraph.

Summary

- A topic sentence states the main idea of a paragraph.
- A topic sentence announces the topic of the paragraph. Usually the topic is found early in the sentence.

- A topic sentence limits the scope of a paragraph. Usually the limiting factor is found in the latter part of the sentence.

- The controlling idea is the specific idea that the paragraph is focused upon.

- A topic sentence can appear at the beginning or the end of the paragraph, or it can be within the paragraph.

- A topic sentence should lead to discussion and elaboration. It should not be an obvious fact. Often topic sentences express attitudes or opinions.

- A good topic sentence presents an idea that is narrow enough to be discussed in one paragraph.

- A good topic sentence is a complete thought. It conveys one dominant idea, not two or more.

- Statements, not questions, make good topic sentences.

- Topic sentences need exact wording, not vague, general wording.

- Topic sentences should present interesting ideas, not stale or boring ideas.

Exercise 3-1:   Evaluating prospective topic sentences

DIRECTIONS: *In each of these pairs of sentences, select the sentence that would make the better topic sentence. Put an* **X** *on the line in front of that sentence. Be prepared to explain your choice in class.*

Example: _____   a. I have enrolled in college because I need to develop skills leading to a better job.

_____**X**_____   b. I have enrolled in Composition 95 because I need excellent writing skills to advance in business.

_____   1. a. Last Saturday, my boyfriend proved how ugly jealousy can be.

_____   1. b. Jealousy can be pretty bad for both people in a relationship.

_____   2. a. I liked having my own apartment, but the expense and responsibility soon became too much.

_____ 2. b. Having my own apartment turned out to be more expensive than I had anticipated.

_____ 3. a. Even though I was fined $350, I learned my lesson about drunk driving in a comparatively easy way.

_____ 3. b. Even though I lost in court, I came out feeling lucky.

_____ 4. a. One evening last summer, Eileen had an unusual experience that was not very pleasant.

_____ 4. b. One evening last summer, Eileen learned how it feels to be robbed.

_____ 5. a. Residents in my community have taken three steps to eliminate pollution from Nine Mile Creek.

_____ 5. b. Someone should do something to clean up water pollution in this state.

_____ 6. a. Fad diets may result in loss of weight, but they can be dangerous.

_____ 6. b. Unbalanced fad diets undermine the dieter's health because they lack essential vitamins and minerals.

_____ 7. a. Janet is a pleasant person to have around.

_____ 7. b. Janet's quick sense of humor eases all of us through tense moments at work.

_____ 8. a. Thousands of teenagers work at fast-food restaurants, but the jobs are not desirable.

_____ 8. b. The manager at Paul's Pizza Palace makes unrealistic demands on employees.

_____ 9. a. Though John Steinbeck and Danielle Steele are both writers with names that start "Ste," they have very different writing styles.

_____ 9. b. American novelists have presented their ideas in a great many ways.

_____ 10. a. Michael learned the hard way that a fifth-grader should stay out of his father's toolbox.

_____ 10. b. Children often get into mischief when they are bored.

Exercise 3-2:   Revising poor topic sentences

DIRECTIONS: *Briefly explain what should be improved in each of these topic sentences. Then write an improved version.*

Example: Being mistaken for someone else can be frightening.

Analysis: The statement should be more specific.
Revision: When I was held as a robbery suspect, I was afraid I would be put in jail.

1. Why would anyone want to cross the Mojave Desert in the middle of July?

   Analysis: _____

   Revision: _____

   _____

2. Repairing boats is an interesting job.

   Analysis: _____

   Revision: _____

   _____

3. My grandma has a heart of gold.

   Analysis: _____

   Revision: _____

   _____

4. A serious problem that threatens the environment.

   Analysis: _____

   Revision: _____

   _____

5. Friendship is the best thing of all.

   Analysis: _____

Revision: _____

_____

6. A person shouldn't rush into anything because haste makes waste.

   Analysis: _____

   Revision: _____

   _____

7. There are many kinds of pets that are fun to have, but I think that cats are the best kind.

   Analysis: _____

   Revision: _____

   _____

8. How do you think I felt when I reached into my pocket and found that my wallet was missing?

   Analysis: _____

   Revision: _____

   _____

9. Thoreau did not believe in accumulating possessions, but rather, he believed in the life of the mind.

   Analysis: _____

   Revision: _____

   _____

10. We should try to save endangered species.

    Analysis: _____

    Revision: _____

    _____

Exercise 3-3:   Forming topic sentences

DIRECTIONS: *Read each of the paragraphs below and decide upon its main idea. Then write an appropriate topic sentence for each one. Put your sentence on the line at the start of the paragraph.*

Paragraph 1

_____

_____

_____

Last summer I took a professional modeling course that included two photographic sessions, classes on makeup application, posture, and wardrobe, and practice in runway performance. I had to attend on my only day off, but it was worth it. We were asked to put together a scrapbook of fashion ideas and our views on modeling as a profession. We had five months to work toward the scrapbook and toward our graduation fashion show. One day in class, we were told that an award would be given for the best runway techniques at the graduation show and another award would be given for the best scrapbook. I decided right away that I was going to win both of these awards. When the day of graduation came, we handed in our projects and went through the performance exactly as we had rehearsed. I thought that I had done well, but when my name was announced as the winner of the trophy for the runway performance, I was very happy. Then I found out that I was also the winner of the best project award, and I was thrilled.

Paragraph 2

_____

_____

_____

Last spring I visited Berlin with my German class. I will never forget standing on the west side of the Brandenburg Gate on a lovely warm evening. We could look from that spot directly into the east side of the city, where people were imprisoned until recently. I stood there in silence for about five minutes. I was remembering the television pictures of East Germans rushing over the wall and through that gate. Soon I felt tears roll down my face, and my teacher came over to talk to me. She said she was sad, too, thinking of what the wall had meant. All the while I was trying to put aside the horrible thoughts of earlier times and concentrate on the present. But since that day I have wondered why a wall had to go up and divide the German people. I have thought a lot about freedom and will never take it for granted again.

Paragraph 3

_____

_____

_____

Some scientists believe that the dinosaurs were killed when a giant asteroid struck the earth. That asteroid may have been several miles in diameter, large enough to throw a tremendous amount of dust and debris into the air. The cloud of dust cut off the sunlight, killing plants and leaving the dinosaurs to starve to death. Other scientists believe that volcanic eruptions changed the atmosphere by throwing tons of smoke and dust into the air. Any massive change in climate that disrupted food supplies could have led to the dinosaurs' extinction. It may be that both asteroids and volcanoes contributed to the fatal change in climate, or some other catastrophe may have caused the death of the dinosaurs.

Paragraph 4

_____

_____

_____

After many years of being at home, I found a job with a book distributor. Within the first few weeks, I knew the job was good for me because I was developing new friends at work. I still see many of these people, even though some of them have left the company. As time passed, I came to appreciate the pay and benefits. I began at $6.25 per hour, but soon I discovered that the company gave small but regular raises to its employees. Another benefit came along after two years. I had the chance to take a training course for supervisors, and it was a great help in understanding people and the business. All this time I was working only a mile and half from home, and so I was able to save both time and gas. But the greatest benefit may have been the job itself. The company sold books of all kinds to schools, public libraries, and universities. With trucks coming continuously, it was Christmas every day. We kept a large stock, and employees were able to borrow or to buy books at a discount. I never got tired of looking at them.

Paragraph 5

_____

_____

_____

I began playing hockey at about age four when my older brothers encouraged me. Starting early was good for me because I could pick up the techniques quickly at that age. Soon I was playing in the Mite League, the first level that beginners play in. Playing well took lots of time and dedication; over many years I worked to build skill in skating and shooting. From grade school through high school, I kept practicing. Many days, as soon as I got home from school, I spent two or three hours shooting pucks in the basement. Most evenings I practiced an hour or more with my friends, and I also went to summer hockey school. By the time I was in high school, I played on the "A" varsity team, the highest level of competition for schools in this state.

Exercise 3-4: Examining placement of topic sentences in paragraphs

DIRECTIONS: *Three versions of one paragraph are written below. The topic sentence is underlined in each paragraph. Notice that in one paragraph the topic sentence is first; in another, it is in the middle, and in the third, it is last.*

Although the topic sentences are not identical, they state essentially the same thing. Read the paragraphs carefully and answer the questions after Example c.

Example a

Though some species of wild birds have been lost forever, for others hope is still alive. One species we have lost is the passenger pigeon. The last of these birds died in the Cincinnati Zoo in 1914. That species was once very common; in fact, by some estimates, passenger pigeons made up 40 percent of the North American bird population in the 1850s. Now that we are more aware, we may be able to save some species, such as the trumpeter swan. By 1938 the trumpeter swan population had fallen to 1,931 birds, and by 1949 only 500 were known to exist in the United States. Today they have increased to about 11,400, a recovery made possible by American citizens' caring intervention. When trumpeter swans were threatened further by drought in 1988, citizens in eastern Idaho raised money for releasing water into reservoirs so as to thaw the rivers and provide water for the swans. Citizens' awareness can make the difference between survival and extinction.

Example b

By the time Americans discovered that some species were in danger of extinction, we had already lost other creatures forever. For instance, the last passenger pigeon died in the Cincinnati Zoo in 1914. That bird was once very common; in fact, by some estimates, passenger pigeons made up 40 percent of the North American bird population in the 1850s. Though some species of wild birds have been lost forever, for others hope is still alive. The trumpeter swan is a good example. By 1938 the trumpeter swan population had fallen to 1,931 birds, and by 1949 only 500 were known in the United States. Today they have increased to about 11,400, a recovery made possible by American citizens' caring intervention. When trumpeter swans were threatened further by drought in 1988, citizens in eastern Idaho raised money to release water into reservoirs so as to thaw the rivers and provide water for the swans. Awareness and intervention can make the difference between survival and extinction.

Example c

When the last passenger pigeon died in the Cincinnati Zoo in 1914, Americans lost a species of wildlife forever. Passenger pigeons had once been very common; in fact, by some estimates, passenger pigeons made up 40 percent of the North American bird population in the 1850s. Belatedly, Americans discovered that some species were threatened and that people would have to intervene to save them. One species we have been able to help is the trumpeter swan. By 1938, the trumpeter swan population had fallen to 1,931 birds, and by 1949 only 500 were known in the United States. Today they have increased to about 11,400, a significant recovery. Citizens have helped in many ways. For instance, when trumpeter swans were further threatened by drought in 1988, citizens in eastern Idaho raised money for releasing water into reservoirs so as to thaw the rivers and provide water for the swans. Though citizens' awareness has made a difference, some species of wild birds have been lost forever, yet for others, hope for survival is still alive.

Opinion Questions

1. Consider only the opening sentences in the three paragraphs. Which of the three openings do you think is most interesting? Why? _____

_____

_____

_____

2. Which opening is most likely to make readers want to learn more? Why?

_____

_____

_____

3. Consider only the last sentences in the three paragraphs. Which of the three endings do you think is most satisfactory? Why? _____

_____

_____

_____

4. Which ending leaves readers with a sense of completion? Why? _____

_____

_____

_____

5. Consider the paragraphs overall. Which of the three is easiest for you to understand? Why? _____

_____

_____

6. Do you see any advantages in putting the topic sentence first in this paragraph? What are they?

_____

_____

_____

Exercise 3-5:   Writing two versions of a paragraph

DIRECTIONS

Part 1:   *On separate paper, write a paragraph using any one of the topic sentences you created in Practice 3-3 above or a revised version of any of the topic ideas in Exercise 3-2 above. Or with your teacher's approval, develop a paragraph on any other topic you like.*

   Underline your topic sentence.

Part 2:   *Revise that paragraph so that your ideas are arranged in another order. Change the wording in your sentences if you wish.*

   Experiment with different placement of your topic sentence. Use the three versions of the paragraph in Exercise 3-4 as examples.

   Underline your topic sentence.

Part 3:   *Bring your paragraphs to class for peer evaluation. To guide your discussion, use the questions at the end of Exercise 1-6 (page 20) or others suggested by your teacher.*

4

Building Support

Balancing General and Specific Statements

General statements are vague because they cover so much territory. You saw examples like these in Chapter 1:

1. a. I like many sports.
1. b. Caffeine can be harmful.
1. c. Construction workers put in long, hard hours.

Specific statements are narrow and exact. For example, the general statements above can be narrowed to these specific statements:

2. a. I play varsity football and basketball during the school year, and I swim and play tennis during the summer.
2. b. Too much caffeine can disturb sleep and cause irritability.
2. c. All summer the electricians worked in the dust and heat, climbing around scaffolding to wire the new office complex.

At first glance, the difference between general and specific statements seems to be their length. Indeed, specific statements usually are longer than general statements, for naturally we need more words to give more details. Contrast statement 1a with its two words, "many sports," and statement 2a with more than twice as many words: "varsity football, basketball, swim, play tennis."

Practice 4-1.   Narrowing general concepts

DIRECTIONS: *Each of these general concepts is narrowed by a specific concept. Add other examples that narrow these general ideas:*

good food __*coleslaw*__

_____

bad habits __*nail biting*__

_____

nice cars __*Lincoln Continentals*__

_____

General words and statements have their place. If you are writing horoscopes or fortune cookies, you will write nothing else. General words and statements leave lots of room for interpretation, and so readers can fill in their own interpretations, just as you and other students did in Practice 4-1. If you compare answers, you will see that your interpretations varied widely.

As you work on your paragraphs, you will often begin with general ideas. Those ideas must be narrowed, just as you narrowed the ideas in Practice 4-1. Expressions like "good food, bad habits, nice cars" can mean many things to different people. You need specific words to express exact meanings, such as coleslaw, nail biting, and Lincoln Continentals. Readers may not agree with your interpretation of "good food," "bad habits," and "nice cars," but they will know exactly what you mean.

Occasionally, specific words and statements carry the entire message. If you are reporting on chemistry experiments, you will write nothing but specific details. Normally, though, you need to balance general and specific words and statements. Try to avoid the beginning writer's tendency to overdo one or the other. Once in a while, but rarely, beginners get too specific and give readers too many details—perhaps details that nobody cares about.

Most of the time, beginners are too general, leaving out too many important details. They may think they are giving readers information, but in fact readers cannot get a clear understanding of their meaning. This student's paragraph leaves readers asking questions such as those in the margin:

topic sentence (When I learned that I was going overseas, I was uneasy about leaving for another country. I was on active duty in the military, and so I had no choice in the decision. I was going to Germany. Before I left, I asked <u>many questions</u> about what it is like to live there. Because I did not know German, I wondered how I would get along off the base. Many of <u>the answers came</u> from sergeants who had lived there. They were <u>positive</u>, and that eased my mind somewhat. Another thing that helped was that others were in for the same culture shock as I was. We all <u>stuck together</u> and tried to think of only the <u>positive side.</u>

Questions like what?

? meaning what?

meaning what?

What answers? What did they say? how?

Practice 4-2. Narrowing general statements

DIRECTIONS: *Write specific statements that could replace the student's general statements. Invent details as you like. Some possible statements are suggested already:*

1. I asked many questions about what it is like to live there.

   I asked about the climate so that I could pack the right clothes for off-duty occasions.

   _____

   _____

   _____

2. Many of the answers came from sergeants who had lived there.

> One sergeant told me that during her twelve-month tour of duty she found the German people friendly and helpful to Americans.

_____

_____

_____

3. They were positive, and that eased my mind somewhat.

> When I learned that Americans were accepted by the Germans, I was reassured.

_____

_____

_____

    In the paragraph below, the student tries to be specific. He leads up to the topic idea stated in the last sentence. All the way along, he uses words that are more concrete than those found in the paragraph above, and the situation is more specific. Even so, the paragraph is still vague and general. Readers would ask questions such as those written in the margin:

What part, exactly?

    This morning I went to the junkyard and removed the <u>interior</u> of a truck. This work included removing the seat, carpet, seatbelts, and door panels. Then I brought all these parts home. I cleaned and vacuumed <u>everything</u> and left <u>it</u> outdoors to dry for a while. Meanwhile I removed the <u>interior of my truck.</u> Then I fitted the new carpet into my truck. Then I added the seatbelts and door panels. Then I put in the seat. Finally I <u>secured everything</u> and cleaned up the mess I had made. Being able to do things like this makes me feel <u>independent and proud of myself.</u>

the same items as listed above

What does "secured everything" mean?

Why?

By contrast, in this next student's paragraph, you will find many specific details. Sentences are numbered for your reference when you analyze the paragraph in Practice 4-3.

[1]When the man walked into the store, I assumed he was looking for a gift for his wife or girlfriend. [2]He browsed for a few minutes, then asked if we had any miniskirts. [3]He added that he wanted hot pink with a ruffle or a flower pattern and that the skirt had to be short because it was for a special event. [4]After searching the store, I found two skirts in the size and style he wanted. [5]When he asked if he could try them on, I was shocked and wanted to laugh, but knew I'd better not. [6]I just mumbled something about where the dressing rooms were. [7]As he went into one of the rooms I realized how glad I was that the store was not very busy. [8]Before long he had dressed and come out to look into the three-way mirror. [9]To my amazement, he asked me how I thought the skirt looked on him. [10]Again I wanted to laugh but realized I didn't dare. [11]I told him that I have always thought that the skirt was cute and that the ruffles have been flattering on everyone who has tried it on. [12]All the while he was turning from side to side to check himself in the mirror. [13]Then he went back to the dressing room, changed, came out, and bought the skirt. [14]I was amazed the whole time, but afterward felt proud of myself for being able to handle an awkward situation like this.

Practice 4-3.   Analyzing a paragraph

DIRECTIONS: *Answer these questions about the paragraph above.*

1. This last paragraph is vivid because of the many specific details. For instance, the customer wanted a miniskirt, specifically in hot pink with ruffles or a floral pattern. List three other vivid details:

    a. _____

    b. _____

    c. _____

2. Several times in the paragraph, the writer mentions moments when she had to weigh her actions and responses. Which sentences refer to her impression that she handled herself well? (Refer to the sentences by

   number.) _____

3. Because this paragraph conveys a clear, exact picture of the situation, we can understand why the writer felt proud. In your own words, what exactly did she have to be proud of? _____

   _____

4. Should the writer have explained further why she felt proud, or has she given enough information to leave us with an understanding of her

   pride? _____

   _____

5. Which is the topic sentence? _____

6. Would the paragraph be stronger if the topic sentence were placed else-

   where in the paragraph? _____ If so, where might it have been

   placed? _____ How would that change in placement improve

   the paragraph? _____

   _____

7. Many readers would consider this last student paragraph the most interesting of the three sample paragraphs in this part of this chapter. Does the interest come from the specific details or from the unusual situation

   or both? _____

   _____

   In a well-written paragraph, a general statement serves as a topic sentence. When the topic sentence is the first sentence in the paragraph, readers know immediately what the paragraph will cover. Sometimes, if a paragraph begins with the topic sentence, it ends with a restatement of the topic idea. That ending statement does *not* merely repeat the topic sentence; it summarizes and sometimes points toward the next paragraph.

Except for the topic sentence and perhaps a concluding sentence, all the other sentences in a paragraph support the topic idea. Those sentences are specific. As the student examples above show, specific statements are essential because they make the meaning clear. Specific statements provide support, and those supporting statements will make up most of the paragraph.

Using Details, Examples, Facts, and Quotations

The most common way to build support in a paragraph is to give detailed information. To find that information, begin by choosing narrow, exact words to explain large, inclusive ones: not good food, but coleslaw or fresh peaches; not bad habits, but nail biting or chewing tobacco. When you start adding details, you may realize that you need to trim down the topic idea.

Usually it is best to cover less and get into more depth. First you might narrow the time and space covered. Suppose that you are writing about your experience as a cashier. Do not write about every job you have had, but focus instead on your current job at a supermarket. Do not write about six months' experience, or even six days' or six hours' experience. Rather, think of a specific situation that occurred within a few minutes.

To show the challenges of your job in sharper detail, you might use a very brief episode. One student did exactly that and wrote this paragraph:

> After two years' experience as a cashier, I've developed a kind of instinct about dishonest people who try to pass bad checks. Recently two women approached my checkout lane with a cart of groceries. I instantly felt uneasy. I rang up their groceries and told one of the women the total, just as usual. She wrote a check and handed it to me. I asked for identification. This is our usual procedure. She gave me her driver's license, and I compared the information on the check with the information on the license. Everything appeared to be okay, and so I thought my instincts were wrong this time. I punched the account number and the amount of the check into the computer, as usual. Then my instincts were confirmed: this check was bad. At that point I called the manager. He explained store policy to the women. He said we could not accept the check because the account had insufficient funds. As they walked away, I was glad that my instincts had alerted me. This awkward situation was easier because I knew what to look for and how to act.

Practice 4-4.   Finding specific support in a paragraph

DIRECTIONS: *Underline specific words and statements in the paragraph above. You might begin with "two women" and "cart of groceries" in the second sentence.*

To use details, simply apply your knowledge of general versus specific words and statements. Being detailed is essentially the same as being specific. The effect is the same: you give readers a clear, exact understanding of what you mean.

Along with details, you might want to use a concrete example or two. Examples can be a great help in showing readers what you mean. You may be able to take examples from your knowledge or experience. If not, you can invent hypothetical examples. Whether truth or fiction, long or short, one or several—examples have one purpose: helping your readers understand by creating a picture in their minds. The student writer who used the bad-check incident created a picture in readers' minds, using details such as those you found in Practice 4-4.

Using examples is not at all subtle. Writers sometimes use "example" or "for example" when giving examples, but of course the word "example" is not necessary because examples usually are too obvious to be overlooked.

In Paragraphs 1 and 2 below, you see different ways in which examples can be presented. In Paragraph 1, the writer does not say "example," but he lists many examples, all in one sentence. In Paragraph 2, the writer mentions examples and then he discusses various examples in separate sentences. As you read, notice that the effect is the same: in both paragraphs the topic idea is explained by the examples.

Paragraph 1

The majority of flowers that grow in vacant lots and along roads are aliens. Hundreds of wayside plants came from Europe. The list is long: Black Mustard, Bouncing Bet, Red Clover, White Clover, Wild Carrot, Spearmint, Peppermint, Mullein, Butter-and-eggs, Teasel, Chicory, Dandelion, Ox-eye Daisy, and many, many others. Some, like the Day-lily of Asia, escaped from gardens, but most came unseen, as seeds mixed in with shipments from across the sea. The first known station for a foreign plant is often at a seaport or along a railroad track.

—Roger Tory Peterson and Margaret McKenny, *A Field Guide to Wildflowers* (Houghton Mifflin, 1968), Introduction, xii.

Paragraph 2

Living things are endowed with a strange and marvelous ability to handle their life activities with a clocklike precision. Potatoes sprout in the bin in February. That is the time for which their built-in chemical alarm is set; December will not do. Lilacs have an appointed time for blooming; no coddling of the plants in a heated greenhouse will change the time. The wild asters by the roadside bloom when the lengthening nights of autumn approach; they seem to wait for these days. Such examples can be extended almost endlessly. Running through them is the general conclusion: each organism has its own built-in timing system.

—Keith G. Irwin, *The 365 Days: The Story of Our Calendar* (Thomas Y. Crowell, 1963), 19–20.

Practice 4-5.   Finding examples in paragraphs

DIRECTIONS: *Underline as many examples as you can find in Paragraphs 1 and 2 above. You might start with "Black Mustard" in Paragraph 1.*

In addition to using details and examples, writers can use facts to support topic sentences. Facts can be drawn from many sources, the most common being newspapers, magazines, and books. By definition, facts are pieces of information about which certainty is possible and about which independent observers will agree. Accurate, up-to-date statistics are one kind of useful fact.

The opposite of fact is opinion, meaning personal interpretation, subject to individual bias. As you know, people may have widely different opinions, even if they otherwise have a lot in common. Writers can express opinions in writing, but to be credible those opinions need to be based upon thorough, objective study of facts or experiences.

Often you will find both facts and opinions in paragraphs and in longer pieces of writing. To find some striking examples of this mixture, look at obituaries, particularly those written long ago. The expected facts are stated, such as the individual's date and place of birth, date and place of marriage, cause of death, and time and place of death. In older obituaries, writers often added their opinions about the individual's personality and character.

Consider the mixture of facts and opinions in this 1888 obituary of a twenty-four-year-old woman:

> **Mrs. Ed. H. Wright.** Finished her earthly life in this city
> on Sabbath, April 29th, Lottie, wife of Mr. E. H. Wright. She

was born at Greenbush, Wis., Dec. 5th, 1863, and was married to Mr. Wright, Jan. 22d, 1884. About a year ago her health began to fail, and soon it was discovered that she was in the relentless grasp of consumption [tuberculosis]. But <u>life was sweet</u>

opinion → <u>to her.</u> In the midst of her relatives; highly respected by all who knew her for her personal worth; popular with her associates, and most tenderly cared for by her husband, it was no easy thing for her to yield, nor did she, until it was clearly seen that the end was only a few hours ahead. Bravely struggling for life, she was taken to California, but not gaining by that, she was brought back to Colorado; here her strong faith in her recovery sustained her for a little time. She would live; she would send for her children; she would have a happy home there. But it was not for her to realize her hope. After a few weeks her husband saw there was little time left for her, and leaving Colorado on Thursday last, they arrived at home on Saturday. . . . Sabbath it was deemed best to tell her that she had but few hours left of life. . . . A husband is bereaved and two little ones are motherless. . . . *St. Cloud [MN] Journal Press,* May 3, 1888.

—From Peg Meier, *Coffee Made Her Insane & Other Nuggets from Old Minnesota Newspapers* (Neighbors Publishing, Minneapolis, MN, 1988), 120.

Practice 4-6. Distinguishing fact from opinion

DIRECTIONS: *Add five items to this list of facts about Lottie Wright.*

She was born in Greenbush, Wisconsin, December 5, 1863.

1. _____

2. _____

3. _____

4. _____

5. _____

Writing in the margins beside the paragraph, mark statements that express opinions. One example has been marked.

You already know some facts that you might use in your writing, and you can easily find many more. For some topics you might consult the dictionary for a basic explanation. The most logical place to look for further information is the library. The resources of your college library will provide you with abundant information on almost any topic. As you think about your topic, watch and listen for relevant information on radio or television, in daily newspapers, and in lectures on campus.

Practice 4-7.   Thinking about sources of facts

DIRECTIONS: *Suppose that you knew only this much about consumption: it was a common killer in the past century, dreaded in those days as cancer is today.*

To write a paragraph about consumption, list three facts you might need:

1. _____

2. _____

3. _____

Name three sources where you would look for the information you need:

1. _____

2. _____

3. _____

Quotations are another useful kind of support. A quotation is a borrowed passage, the exact words of a writer or speaker. When writing, you may borrow, provided you give credit to the source. Taking someone's exact words—or even paraphrasing someone's ideas—without giving credit is plagiarism, a form of stealing. To be honest, you must identify your source. Besides giving the name of the source, you might indicate that person's authority by including a title or position. Of course, if the source is likely to be well known to your readers, identification is not necessary.

If the quotation is brief, put quotation marks around the borrowed words: President Lincoln began, "Fourscore and seven years ago our fathers brought forth on this continent a new nation...." " In paragraph writing, you generally name the source (the person or the publication) in the same sentence, as shown in this paragraph with President Lincoln's statement.

If the borrowed passage is longer than four lines, set the entire passage apart and indent; leave space above and below the quoted passage. Do not use quotation marks here, for the spacing on the page shows that the passage is quoted. The borrowed paragraphs you find in this book are examples.

Well-selected quotations are vivid and interesting. Because they are someone's direct words, they seem immediate and close. Naturally, the more colorful or distinctive the words are, the more they stand out.

You do not have to quote famous words from famous people to get these effects; quotations can serve your purpose even if they come from "ordinary people." In this passage, a student quotes her friend's words to make the situation vivid and to reveal her friend's attitudes:

> Darlene and I have been friends for nearly five years, but until yesterday, I guess I didn't understand her. We were having breakfast, as we normally did every Saturday, at a nearby restaurant. I don't know what we found to talk about all those Saturdays, but kids, husbands, jobs, and life in general were covered.
>
> Nothing seemed out of the ordinary yesterday until Darlene slowly looked up from her plate and said, "Julie, you don't see anything wrong with me, do you? Well, there is. I can't eat. I can't sleep. I can't think straight. I suppose you might as well know. My son's on drugs, Julie. My little Mikey—I'll say it. How am I going to live through this?"
>
> I looked up at her, startled and amazed, and I wondered what to say. Before I even got a chance to say a thing, she continued, half whispering. "You're the first person I've even *dared* breathe a word to about this, outside our family. I don't know what to do. It's tearing me apart—well, you can see it in my eyes. I barely slept last night. I really need help." She dropped her fork on her plate with a definite CLANK! a kind of announcement to the world. She had a determined look in her eyes, too. I know that look.
>
> I sat there for what seemed like an hour, holding a forkful of eggs benedict in midair. While I was thinking, she said, "Here, use my napkin."

I was unaware of the hollandaise sauce dripping onto my lap. Because I didn't know what to say, I just nodded. Somehow, I managed to set my fork down, swallow a bite of food, and wipe the sauce off my slacks. Darlene paid no attention but kept looking down at her plate. Finally I said something, maybe the wrong thing, but the only thing I could think of: "But what about him? What about Mike?"

Practice 4-8. Finding support in paragraphs

DIRECTIONS: *Answer these questions about the example above.*

Besides the quotations, name five details that help you picture the situation described in the passage:

1. _____

2. _____

3. _____

4. _____

5. _____

Name three facts included in this passage:

1. _____

2. _____

3. _____

What is the main idea? _____

_____

In your opinion, would the passage have been better in one paragraph? Why or why not? _____

_____

_____

The examples above show that writers combine details, examples, facts, and quotations to support their main ideas. There is no one "right" way to select and use these supporting elements. The main goal is to make the support relevant and adequate. More often than not, several kinds of support are needed to develop a main idea.

Summary

- Paragraphs carry both general and specific statements. A comparatively general statement is used for a topic sentence. The other sentences should be much more specific.

- Details provide support. Details are specific pieces of information that show what the writer means by the topic sentence.

- Examples illustrate a main idea. One or more examples might be useful, depending upon the general idea being supported.

- Facts are statements about which independent observers agree. Opinions are personal interpretations of facts. Both facts and opinions are used in paragraphs.

- Quotations are the exact words of a writer or speaker.

- Short quotations (no more than four lines) are set off with quotation marks.

- Long quotations (more than four lines) are indented and set apart as a block on the page.

- Most paragraphs combine devices for support, including details, examples, facts, and quotations.

Exercise 4-1:   Creating specific support

DIRECTIONS: *For each of these general concepts, create specific supporting ideas. Examples are given in each instance.*

1. *General:*   an interesting but frightening experience
   Specific: climbing Half Dome, a mountain at Yosemite National Park

   _____

   _____

   _____

2. *General:*   a person who made me think of a character on television
   Specific: The large man ordered the biggest meal on the menu, reminding me of Norm Peterson in "Cheers," ordering a platter of food at the Hungry Heifer.

   _____

   _____

   _____

3. *General:*   a dangerous stretch to drive
   Specific: a two-lane gravel road winding up the side of a mountain with no guardrails between the edge of the road and the cliff

   _____

   _____

   _____

4. *General:*   an unusual hairstyle
   Specific: the head shaved on both sides and in back, with the hair on top cut short, dyed purple, and made to stand up like a rooster's comb

   _____

   _____

   _____

5. *General:* a punishment that seems too lenient

   Specific: a $500 fine and 200 hours of community service for each of the vandals who did $2,000,000 in damage to a public high school

_____

_____

_____

6. *General:* a well-equipped, low-priced used car

   Specific: a sports car with AM/FM radio, stereo system consisting of four speakers and autoreverse tape player, automatic transmission, for $1,400

_____

_____

_____

7. *General:* a great restaurant bargain

   Specific: breakfast for $1.99, consisting of two eggs (scrambled or fried to order), hash browns, 6 oz. strip steak cooked to order, and wheat toast with butter and jelly

_____

_____

_____

8. *General:* a large wedding

   Specific: bride and groom with four attendants each, plus flower girl and ring bearer; three-hundred guests

_____

_____

_____

9. *General:* a famous scientist

 Specific: physicist Stephen Hawking, author of *A Brief History of Time* and professor at Cambridge University, England

_____

_____

_____

10. *General:* a challenging college course

 Specific: Problem Solving and Computer Design 3311

_____

_____

_____

Exercise 4-2:   Adding details, examples, facts, and quotations

DIRECTIONS: *Select any five of the general statements listed here. Provide specific details, examples, facts, and quotations that support each general statement. Write on separate paper.*

Example

General: The elderly man seemed sad, but probably he was frustrated by loneliness and helplessness.

Specific: An elderly man was standing by the canned vegetables as I came along with my grocery cart. I was walking past him when he spoke to me. "My wife bought the best-tasting canned peas, but she died, and I don't know what brand they were. What do you think would be good?" I looked at him, then glanced away because I felt uneasy, seeing tears in his eyes and hearing his voice start to shake. I knew he was not as troubled about canned peas as he was about being alone and having to deal with details of life that he had never thought about before.

1. The landlord does not keep up our building.

2. Learning English was difficult for me when I first got to this country. (Use any second language that you have learned, mentioning the circumstances.)

3. That accident proved to me how important seatbelts are.

4. Working in a fast-food restaurant is harder than it looks.

5. Managers sometimes make unreasonable demands on employees.

6. Firefighters have to deal with life-threatening situations routinely, whether they are fighting fires in the forest or in a building.

7. Despite medical advances and changes in lifestyle, heart disease remains the leading cause of death in the United States.

8. Being a single parent is hard.

9. Living on welfare is hard.

10. Dealing with a domestic dispute can be very dangerous for police officers.

Exercise 4-3: Identifying main ideas

DIRECTIONS: *To get a message across to readers, we sometimes have to study a set of facts and come up with the main idea—the "big picture"—and then use the facts to support that idea. Four sets of facts are presented below. For each, think carefully about all the facts, then write a sentence summing up the main idea.*

Example

Facts: Roger Twain leads the league with a 1.86 ERA. He also has fifteen shutouts on the year, and he is undefeated with a 17-0 mark. His strikeout-to-walk ratio is roughly ten (200/23), and opposing batters are hitting .075 against him.

Main idea: Pitcher Roger Twain has an exceptional record.

Problem 1

Facts: My new radio has a digital clock, a digital alarm, and an AM/FM radio. It also picks up the audio on VHF television channels, and it has an autoreverse tape player. It also has a telephone with two lines, a built-in answering machine for both, and an automatic redial feature.

Main idea: _____

_____

_____

Problem 2

Facts: As of July 1989, New Mexico's population was 38 percent Hispanic. The population of Texas was 28 percent Hispanic, slightly higher than California's standing at 22 percent. New Mexico's percentage of Hispanic residents is the highest in the nation. Besides New Mexico, Texas, and California, states with significant Hispanic populations are Arizona (17 percent), Colorado (12 percent), New York (11 percent), and Florida (10 percent). Other states have smaller percentages. (Source: U.S. Bureau of the Census, as quoted in *The Fresno Bee*, Fresno, CA, July 5, 1989)

Main idea: _____

_____

_____

Problem 3

Facts: Leprosy is one of humanity's oldest diseases. It still affects millions of people, particularly in the third world, but 5,000 cases have been found in the United States. Less than 3 percent of the world's population is susceptible. Leprosy is caused by bacteria spread through nasal mucus. Only those who have prolonged contact with victims are likely to become infected. The disease is dreaded because it causes grotesque deformities, especially of the face and limbs.

Main idea: _____

_____

_____

Problem 4

Facts: Music was first accepted as part of a public-school curriculum in Boston in 1838. After that, every grammar-school child was taught to read music and sing. Supporters of music had worked hard to overcome public objections. Some taxpayers said that because music was a rare gift, teaching music to all children would be a waste. Besides, according to them, music is frivolous. Education is about reading, writing, and arithmetic. A Boston musician named Lowell Mason had taught during the previous year without salary, proving that all children could learn to sing and disproving objections.

Main idea: _____

_____

_____

Exercise 4-4:   Finding support in paragraphs

DIRECTIONS: *These students' paragraphs rely upon details, examples, facts, and quotations. Some instances of these kinds of support are marked in the margins. Read carefully, and mark as many other instances as you can find. Underline the topic sentence in each paragraph.*

Paragraph 1

Though nobody knows what causes stuttering, there are three common theories. A popular one suggests that stress is the culprit. In nervous people, stuttering is explained away by

quotation (statements like, "Oh, he's stuttering because he can't take the heat." Most stutterers wish it were that simple. Although stress

fact (can contribute to an existing problem, experts have proved that stress by itself cannot cause stuttering. Another theory is role conflict, which suggests that stuttering occurs only when the person is in a particular role. Jeff, who works at Hardee's, is

example | a good example. When a pretty girl walks in and places an order, Jeff sounds fine because she's just another customer. But when Jeff meets that same girl at a party, he struggles from sentence to sentence because he's in a different role. The third theory suggests that stutterers in general are more defensive than nonstutterers, but there is no proof that defensiveness causes stuttering. The theories are only theories, and to this day we do not know the cause.

Paragraph 2

On my sixteenth birthday, my grandparents gave me the

details (ugliest necktie I had ever seen. It was brown with large, *details*

bright-yellow polkadots. It was about fourteen inches long. The tie was narrow at the top, then spread out to a five-inch triangular base. It was one of those fashionable clip ties that need no tying. When I fastened it on my shirt, it hung from my neck like a cowbell. I remember feeling my face turn red and thinking that I now knew the meaning of the words "disgust" and "embarrassment." The hardest part was trying not to hurt my grandparents' feelings. They were watching me and smiling the kind of smiles that could melt frozen butter at a glance. When I got the tie on, they said, in tune with each other, "That's our grandson!" I didn't think I could feel much worse, but then they thought of taking pictures. Somehow I got through a photo session with forced smiles on my face. Even now I don't know how I kept smiling. I found that I could control my own emotions to spare someone else's feelings, although it wasn't easy.

Paragraph 3

quotation

My saddest memories come from a time when I was not quite seven years old. Though I was young, I learned that my dad had great strength and courage. I remember the night he was pacing back and forth in our house. He didn't say much, but finally he whispered to me, "Son, we're going to move to Thailand." I did not understand what he meant, but from the look on his face I knew he was deeply troubled by what was going on. Before long, our family began the journey. We were going with other Vietnamese who wanted freedom. I sensed that my dad was the leader. We had not traveled far when we came upon some communist troops patrolling the riverfront. They started shooting at us, and we fled into the woods. When we regrouped, we learned that they had killed fifteen of the thirty-five people in our party. I heard my dad say something about my mother and my older brother. Suddenly I realized what had happened, and in my anger I started running back to the river, but Dad caught up with me and made me return with him. Later, in Thailand, we met other refugees, people who came after us. Many years afterward, Dad told me that they had found my mother's body and with her, my brother.

Exercise 4-5:   Writing a paragraph

DIRECTIONS: *On separate paper, write a paragraph on a topic of your choice, a topic suggested by any of the exercises in this chapter, or a topic suggested by your teacher. Experiment with using details, examples, facts, and quotations—individually or in any combination that works. Underline your topic sentence. With your teacher's approval, write notes in the margins, pointing out your details, examples, facts, opinions, and quotations.*

Use this paragraph for peer evaluation. Focus particularly on the quality of support in the paragraph.

Exercise 4-6:   Revising a paragraph

DIRECTIONS: *Revise a paragraph you wrote earlier in this course, perhaps one written in response to exercises in another chapter. Your goal is to improve the support. Add details, examples, facts, and quotations individually or in any combination that works.*

Turn in your original paragraph and the revised version.

5

Providing Coherence

Understanding Coherence

A good paragraph has **coherence**, meaning that all the sentences flow smoothly from one to another and the relationships between ideas are clear. In coherent writing, relevant supporting ideas explain previous statements. Connecting words join related ideas, or make smooth transitions into contrasting ideas. Main ideas are easy to follow because of repetition and variation of key words and concepts.

One way to understand coherence is to think about what happens when it is absent. Coherence is like other qualities we don't notice unless they aren't there. For example, we may not notice air conditioning until we step outdoors into a steam bath of humidity. We don't think about courtesy until we are treated rudely. We don't think about finding our way until we get lost. Similarly, we don't think about coherence until we run into incoherence.

As a reader, you will recognize incoherence when you see it. You will be lurching from one idea to another, trying to follow rambling, disjointed statements. Reading incoherent writing is like riding with a driver who is lost, who wanders up and down bumpy side streets, hunting for a destination but wasting time and jarring passengers around.

Here is an example of incoherent writing:

[1]I wouldn't describe one of my days as typical. [2]Many people have hectic lives from day to day. [3]Two weeks ago my life took on an accelerated pace. [4]I used to wake up around noon and take a few classes. [5]I started work at a construction job. [6]The money is good, better than I

used to get at a fast-food restaurant. [7]I am a painter. [8]My day begins before sunup. [9]After working all morning, I squeeze in a history class during my lunch hour. [10]Then I work all afternoon. [11]I don't even like history, but my adviser told me to take a history course. [12]By the time I'm off work in the afternoon, I am really tired. [13]I do a lot of climbing on ladders. [14]Then I'm homeward bound, and traffic is sometimes tied up, or I get behind slow-moving vehicles. [15]When we have snow, even an inch or so, the traffic is still worse. [16]After dinner I try to get some homework done, or I just fall asleep. [17]By then it's hard to read a history book. [18]I just recently accepted the fact that I'm no longer Mom and Dad's little girl. [19]I took it upon myself to move out on my own. [20]I guess I never appreciated all those things my family did for me when I was younger. [21]Now I know how hard people must work to survive in this world.

Practice 5-1. Examining an incoherent paragraph

DIRECTIONS: *Answer these questions about the paragraph above.*

1. Which sentences might be considered as possible topic sentences?

   _____

2. Which sentences pertain to the writer's job?

   _____

3. Which sentences pertain to the writer's schooling?

   _____

4. Aside from the job and school, list three topics the writer mentions briefly.

   a. _____

   b. _____

   c. _____

5. Name a spot in the paragraph where one sentence does not flow well from the one before.

   _____

6. Which sentences seem unrelated to the topic of the paragraph?

_____

By contrast, consider the student paragraph below. You read this paragraph in Chapter 1, but at that time you were not thinking about coherence. Now notice how smoothly the writer takes us from sentence to sentence, and notice that the writer shows us exactly how each idea, detail, or example is related to what precedes it.

notice the repeating of coin and collecting and synonyms

notice the repeated "ing" forms

dad... grandpa... (a pattern repeated)

connects ideas

connects past to future

notice use of examples

[1]For most of my life I have been fascinated with coins. [2]As far back into my childhood as I can remember, I recall looking at coins, handling them, and reading the dates on them. [3]I started collecting coins when I turned seven, and I've been collecting them ever since. [4]When my family saw how serious my interest was, my dad bought me coin-holder books, and my grandpa gave me his entire collection. [5]As a teenager I saved money from my weekly allowance and my paper route so that I could buy more coins. [6]With each purchase I wrote down the name of the coin, its date, condition, and type. [7]Now I have a valuable collection with about 500 coins. [8]My oldest coin is a 1798 large cent penny, and my two newest coins, part of a set, are 1988 proof silver one-dollar and half-dollar commemoratives. [9]To this day, when I have time, I go to the bank and buy rolls of pennies, nickels, or dimes, and search for rare coins. [10]My immediate goal is to build a collection of about 1,500 coins over the next five years. [11]Eventually I hope to pass along my interest and my collection to children of my own.

Practice 5-2.   Examining a coherent paragraph

DIRECTIONS: *Answer these questions about the paragraph above.*

1. The topic sentence is sentence 1. What is the controlling idea in this paragraph? _____

2. Which sentences pertain to the writer's early childhood experiences?

   _____

3. Which sentences pertain to the writer's collection? _____

4. Name one spot in the paragraph where consecutive sentences are so closely related that the second seems to follow naturally from the first.

   _____

5. The writer guides readers through the paragraph by using chronological order. At which places in the paragraph do you notice that you are moving ahead in time? _____

   _____

   Coherence is an important quality, as you can see by contrasting the paragraphs above. Even so, coherence has not been mentioned earlier in this book. The reason is simply this: you will think more about coherence **after** finding topics, forming main ideas, and building support. Rough drafts will have some coherence, assuming you stay on your topic. Mainly, though, it is while revising that you will examine the relationships of ideas and refine wording to ensure coherence.

   You can sense that coherence comes partly from staying on the topic, partly from organizing logically, and partly from wording statements carefully. The rest of this chapter shows you specific ways to ensure coherence. The devices are numerous and varied, but the quality is measured by several tests. You can use these questions to test the coherence in your paragraphs:

   - Do all these ideas belong here?
   - Are the relationships and connections between the ideas clear?
   - Does every sentence follow naturally from the one before?
   - Does the writing—in total—hold together as a logical, understandable unit?

Using Devices to Ensure Coherence

Paragraph writers connect ideas by using these devices:

- transitional words, phrases, and clauses
- pronoun reference
- parallelism
- repetition of key words and concepts

Transitional Words, Phrases, and Clauses

Words, phrases, and clauses used as transitions are like bridges that carry readers safely from one point to another. Writers finish one complete thought at a time and stop, and they signal that stop with an ending mark (usually a period) at the end of the sentence. Readers need to connect those individual sentences. To help them do so, writers sometimes put in a bridge to carry them across the "space" between ideas. Some of the most frequently used bridges are the seven conjunctions used with commas to join related independent thoughts:

for, and, nor, but, or, yet, so

Examples: I started collecting coins when I turned seven, and I've been collecting them ever since.
Debra worked only a block from home, so she saved both time and money by walking to work.

When complete thoughts are closely related, they can be joined with semicolons. Immediately after semicolons, writers often use bridges like these, leading into the next complete thought:

therefore	however	moreover
consequently	nevertheless	conversely
even so	nonetheless	in fact
in addition	by contrast	on the contrary
on the other hand	for instance	for example

Examples: The customer had proper identification; however, a check with the computer showed that her account was overdrawn. (Note: "However" leads to a contrasting idea; it reverses the direction of thought. Here it reverses expectations set up in the first independent clause.)

The computer showed that the customer's account had been closed; consequently, the cashier could not accept her check. (Note: "Consequently" calls attention to a cause-and-effect relationship between the ideas.)

The earthquake hit at rush hour; nevertheless, most commuters managed to get home safely.
(Note: "Nevertheless" leads to a reassuring second statement; "even so" and "nonetheless" have the same effect.)

In these examples the underlined introductory word groups (dependent clauses and prepositional phrases) serve as transitions:

As far back into childhood as I can remember, I recall looking at coins.
As a teenager I saved money from my allowance. . . .
When my family saw how serious my interest was, my dad bought me
    coin-holder books. . . .

Many words and phrases can be used as transitions. Textbooks list common transitions, but dozens of other expressions can serve as transitions as well. Of course, transitions are not always found at the same places in sentences. Many times they are used with commas or semicolons between complete thoughts, but they can appear elsewhere in sentences. For instance, these transitions can be used at the start of a sentence, within a sentence, or immediately after a semicolon, as a bridge into a new thought:

then, later, thereafter, soon after	(to signal the passing of time)
first, second, third, last	(to enumerate)
in summary, in conclusion, in short	(to signal the end)
as a consequence, in fact, indeed	(to emphasize or point out)

In the two paragraphs below, some of the transitions are italicized. Two paragraphs are shown here because it is important to recognize that transitions are used **between** paragraphs as well as within paragraphs. The principle is exactly the same: providing bridges so that readers can move easily from one thought to another.

Though I   had studied Spanish in school, the classroom didn't prepare me for the reality I ran into recently. I was traveling through a small town in California when I went into Mountain Mike's Pizza Parlor for food. There was a pool table in the corner, *and so* to kill time while waiting for my pizza, I started shooting. *Before long,* the man who had taken my order came over to watch. *Glancing up,* I thought he looked Hispanic, so I asked him, "¿Qué tal?" which means "How's it going?" He looked at me wide-eyed, then began to speak to me in Spanish. As we chatted, all in Spanish, I learned that he was the owner and that his name was Miguel. Now, in fact, white guys speaking Spanish didn't impress Miguel very much; after all, that is pretty common in California.

Instead, what really impressed Miguel was my pool game. *Actually,* I am a fairly good player, but he was gasping every time I made a tougher-than-average shot, and we weren't playing for anything at all. Soon he told me that I was better than anyone he'd seen and that I should be at Frankie's Billiards. *Furthermore,* he said that was where all the good players went. Reminding him that I was just traveling through, I asked him, "¿Por qué no vas a Frankie's?" In other words, "Why don't you go to Frankie's?" Then I got a real surprise, *for* Miguel explained to me that Hispanics aren't welcome in some establishments, that being one. Studying Spanish in school had not prepared me for a first-hand encounter with stupid, blind prejudice.

Practice 5-3. Finding transitions

DIRECTIONS: *Underline at least six more transitional words and phrases in the two paragraphs above.*

Pronoun Reference

Words used as pronoun references tie ideas together because of the way pronouns work. Let's review for a moment: Some of the most common pronouns refer directly to specific persons, such as *I, me, you, he, him, she, her, they,* and *them.* Some other common pronouns refer less directly to people or things, including *it, one, someone, somebody, anyone,* and *anybody.*

Pronouns pick up their meaning in context: they take their meaning from the person(s) or things(s) referred to. Normally a noun is nearby—in the same sentence or in a nearby sentence—to provide a reference that gives meaning to the pronoun. Notice the connections between the noun "commuters" and the pronouns "they" and "their" in these sentences:

noun

While the commuters were driving home, <u>they</u> saw the highway buckle. Immediately <u>they</u> began pulling over to stop. Within moments <u>they</u> realized an earthquake had struck <u>their</u> city, San Francisco.

Because pronouns refer to nearby nouns, automatic connections are made, and those connections tie sentences together. The student paragraph below appeared in Chapter 1, but as you read it this time, watch for the pronouns. Notice, for instance, how sentences 5 and 6 are connected by the pronoun–noun relationship:

[1]I learned early in life that I had to be more patient and less aggressive. [2]From the time I was about four years old until I was about six, I was a destructive person. [3]My parents bought me toys, and I was happy as long as the toys worked. [4]But when things went wrong, I got frustrated and angry and sometimes broke the toys. [5]For a while my parents bought me new toys. [6]But before long they began to see what was happening. [7]On my fifth birthday they bought me an electric train set. [8]Within a few weeks I smashed it because a short in the wiring had cut the power. [9]My parents said, "That's it! [10]No more toys for you for a long time." [11]About a year later my punishment ended. [12]Meanwhile, I found out that with more patience I could make my toys last. [13]I found out that I had fewer problems with things breaking. [14]My attitude changed from then on.

Practice 5-4.   Analyzing a paragraph

DIRECTIONS: *Underline transitional words and phrases in the paragraph above.*

1. Which is the topic sentence? _____

2. Name two kinds of support that the writer used.
   (Consider the kinds of support discussed in Chapter 4.)

   a. _____

   b. _____

3. What is the pronoun–noun connection between sentences 5 and 6?

   _____

Parallelism

Parallel wording means deliberate repetition of word patterns. It ties ideas together, as you see in these examples:

infinitives   To be or not to be: that is the question. (Shakespeare, *Hamlet,* Act III)

prepositional phrases   ...government of the people, by the people, for the people.... (President Lincoln)

independent clauses   Ask not what your country can do for you; ask what you can do for your country. (President Kennedy)

Parallelism has been used for centuries. This famous example comes from the Declaration of Independence, 1774:

three "that" Clauses   We hold these truths to be self-evident, that all men are created equal, that they are endowed by their Creator with certain inalienable Rights, that among these are Life, Liberty, and the pursuit of Happiness....

The King James version of the Bible (1611) has many examples, including this one:

complete thoughts ←— In the morning it is green and groweth up; but in the evening it is cut down, dried up, and withered. (Psalm 90:6) —→ *verbs*

Paragraph writers use parallelism to connect ideas in readers' minds. The repetition makes the connections automatic in much the same way as pronoun–noun reference does. Most of the time, parallelism, transitional words and phrases, and pronoun–noun reference are used in combination to ensure coherence.

Repetition of Key Words

One additional device is used to gain coherence: repeating key words or concepts, using those very words or synonyms of those words. In a way, this "device" is related not so much to coherence as to staying on the topic. Writers who stay on their topics are sure to repeat the main words and concepts pertaining to those topics, though not always with the very same words.

Here is an analysis of a student's paragraph you found in Exercise 4-4. In this paragraph the student uses repetition of the term "stuttering" and variations of that word, and also uses repetition of the word "theory." The other devices described above are also found here:

[1]Though nobody knows what causes stuttering, there are (three) common theories. [2]A popular (one) suggests that stress is the culprit. [3]In nervous people, stuttering is explained away by statements like, "Oh, he's stuttering because he can't take the heat." [4]Most stutterers wish it were that simple. [5]Although stress can contribute to a problem, experts have proved that stress by itself cannot cause stuttering. [6]Another theory is role conflict, which suggests that stuttering occurs only when the person is in a particular role. [7]Jeff, who works at Hardee's, is a good example. [8]When a pretty girl walks in and places an order, Jeff sounds fine because she's just another customer. [9]But when Jeff meets that same girl at a party, he struggles from sentence to sentence because he's in a different role. [10]The (third) theory suggests that stutterers in general are more defensive than nonstutterers, but there is no proof that defensiveness causes stuttering. [11]The theories are only theories, and to this day we do not know the cause.

notice enumerating of the three theories

transition

and repetition of "theory" and "stuttering"

Practice 5-5. Analyzing a paragraph for coherence

DIRECTIONS: *In Exercise 4-4, you examined this paragraph to discover how the student supported his main idea. Now examine the paragraph to see how he ensured coherence:*

[1]On my sixteenth birthday my grandparents gave me the ugliest necktie I had ever seen. [2]It was brown with large, bright-yellow polkadots. [3]It was about fourteen inches long. [4]The tie was narrow at the top, then spread out to a five-inch triangular base. [5]It was one of those fashionable clip ties that need no tying. [6]When I fastened it on my shirt, it hung from my neck like a cowbell. [7]I remember feeling my face turn red and thinking that I now knew the meaning of the words "disgust" and "embarrassment." [8]The hardest part was trying not to hurt my grandparents' feelings. [9]They were watching me and smiling the kind of smiles that could melt frozen butter at a glance. [10]When I got the tie on, they said, in tune with each other, "That's our grandson!" [11]I didn't think I could feel much worse, but then they thought of taking pictures. [12]Somehow I got through a photo session with forced smiles on my face. [13]Even now I don't know how I kept smiling. [14]I found that I could control my own emotions to spare someone else's feelings, but it wasn't easy.

1. Underline transitional words and phrases in the paragraph.

2. Connect nouns and pronouns with arrows, just as you see in the paragraph above about stuttering.

3. Which sentences use parallelism? _____

4. Which key words are repeated in this paragraph?

_____

As a writer, you have several devices to help you attain coherence. You can use these devices whenever and wherever you believe they help. You can—and generally should—use these devices in combination. But above all else, work to connect your ideas, showing relationships and smoothing the way for your readers.

Summary

- Paragraph coherence means that all the sentences flow smoothly from one to another, and the ideas are connected so that the relationships between them are clear.

- Transitional words, phrases, and clauses connect ideas. They carry readers from one idea to another smoothly.

- The conjunctions used with a comma to connect independent ideas are common transitions. These conjunctions are *for, and, nor, but, or, yet, so.*

- Transitional words are sometimes used with semicolons to connect independent ideas. Common examples of these transitional words are *however, therefore, consequently, moreover, nevertheless.*

- Transitional words and phrases sometimes enumerate (*first, second, last*), sometimes signal an ending (*in conclusion, in summary, in short*), sometimes emphasize (*in fact, indeed*), and sometimes point to examples (*for instance, for example*).

- Pronoun reference connects ideas because pronouns refer to nearby nouns.

- Parallelism connects ideas by repetition of a word pattern in a sentence or within a series of sentences.

- Repetition of key words or concepts ties a paragraph together by keeping readers' attention focused on the key idea.

- Writers use a combination of devices—transitional words, phrases, and clauses; pronoun–noun reference; parallelism; and repetition of key words—to ensure coherence.

Exercise 5-1: Looking for related ideas

DIRECTIONS: *Read each set of sentences and consider how the ideas are related. Then follow these steps:*

 a. *For each set of sentences, find a main idea that most of the sentences support. Write that idea on the line that follows the sentences.*

 b. *Put a line through the one sentence that does not pertain to the others or to the main idea.*

Example: a. I worked on a construction crew last summer.
 b. ~~The big tuition increase this year will take all my savings from the summer.~~
 c. I had a hard job, carrying heavy packs of shingles in the heat.
 d. The crew started work soon after dawn to avoid the hottest part of the day.

 Main idea: my summer job in construction

1. a. Though the owner's real name was Miguel, his nickname was Mountain Mike.

 b. Miguel and I spoke in Spanish and played pool.

 c. Miguel's friends, Manuel and Jaime, stood and watched.

 d. My pool playing was more impressive to them than my textbook Spanish.

 Main idea: _____

 _____

2. a. About ten years ago I had hepatitis.

 b. Besides being very tired, I had yellow skin, could eat almost nothing, and felt very weak.

 c. In the hospital I slept a lot and had blood tests every four hours.

 d. After I left the hospital, I learned that my employer had assigned many of my duties to others.

 Main idea: _____

 _____

3. a. Car travel is easier on pets than is air travel.

   b. Airlines will generally not allow puppies and kittens younger than eight weeks to fly.

   c. Make sure that your pet is restrained in the car, because an animal that crawls under the brake pedal causes hazards.

   d. Stop often and let your pet walk around outside for a few minutes.

   Main idea: _____

   _____

4. a. American painter Gilbert Stuart, who completed about 1,000 portraits, is best remembered for his portraits of George Washington.

   b. Gilbert Stuart's daughter, Jane, and other artists of the next generation imitated Stuart's style.

   c. Gilbert Stuart (1755–1828) was praised by his contemporaries, and his work is still admired.

   d. Virginian Jeb Stuart, a distinguished Confederate officer in the War Between the States, was not related to Gilbert Stuart.

   Main idea: _____

   _____

5. a. Charles Darwin disappointed his physician father by failing his pre-med courses in college.

   b. The turning point in Darwin's life was his long voyage on HMS *Beagle*.

   c. The purpose of the *Beagle*'s trip was scientific exploration, and Darwin went along as a naturalist.

   d. The voyage took Darwin to the Southern Hemisphere, including the Galápagos Islands, where he collected hundreds of specimens for study.

   Main idea: _____

   _____

6. a. Hoover Dam, built in the 1930s, was planned as a means of controlling the Colorado River.

   b. Frequent spring floods had destroyed homes and crops in the river valley.

c. Hoover Dam was originally named Boulder Dam.

d. The dam allowed for restraining flood waters and for diverting water into irrigation canals.

Main Idea: _____

_____

7. a. In 1864, President Lincoln granted the state of California a parcel of land that later became part of Yosemite National Park.

b. Even before that time, visitors were drawn to the area by its natural beauty, and hotels had been built to accommodate them.

c. In recent years, the park service banned the gathering of firewood in an effort to lessen the effect of campfires and smoke on the natural environment.

d. The present 1,183-square-mile park was established as Yosemite National Park in 1890.

Main idea: _____

_____

Exercise 5-2:   Revising sentences to show relationships of ideas

DIRECTIONS: *Revise the statements in each group below so that the ideas are smoothly connected and the relationships of ideas are made clear. You may change the wording, but preserve the meaning. Or you may leave the present wording, but add transitional words or phrases.*

Example

Problem: I knew how to speak Spanish from taking it in school. The classroom didn't prepare me for the reality I ran into recently. I was traveling through Bakersfield, California.

Revision: Though I had studied Spanish in school, the classroom didn't prepare me for the reality I ran into recently while traveling through Bakersfield, California.

or

I knew how to speak Spanish from taking it in school; however, the classroom didn't prepare me for the reality I ran into recently in Bakersfield, California.

1. I did nothing but sleep during my first two days in the hospital. I was very weak. I was constantly tired, no matter how much I slept.

   _____

   _____

   _____

2. The doctor came in a couple of times a day. She read my chart. She asked me questions. Her attention made me uneasy. Was she that worried about me? I wondered how sick I really was.

   _____

   _____

   _____

   _____

3. The blood tests made me lightheaded. I almost fainted a couple of times. I couldn't think clearly.

   _____

   _____

4. Some foods tasted awful. Milk and milk products tasted awful. For many days I was sick to my stomach.

   _____

   _____

5. You will see many things when you take your motorcycle driving test. You will see tight curves and electronic timing devices. You will notice black tire marks on the roadway. You will also see the examiner's cold stare.

   _____

   _____

   _____

   _____

6. I saw the red light come on. I hit the brakes. The cycle skidded to a stop. I was just outside the white lines. I knew I had just failed my test.

_____

_____

_____

7. During class I daydreamed about my date. I planned it all out. I thought of everything. I began by asking Jennie out. I ended up getting a good-night kiss. We would eat and see a movie. It would be on Saturday night.

_____

_____

_____

_____

8. I would pick her up right on time. She would be waiting for me. We would go to a steak house on the east side of town. The food there is affordable but nice.

_____

_____

_____

Exercise 5-3: Examining transitions in a short essay

DIRECTIONS: *Underline the transitions in the student writing below. Remember that transitions can be used between paragraphs as well as within paragraphs; they are also used within sentences as well as between sentences.*

I was a couple of days past sixteen, and I had just gotten my driver's license. By that time, I had thought about Jennie a lot. She was a really special girl, and I was waiting for that special moment. Now it looked like it was here. I could finally drive the family car, and so I was ready to ask her for that special date that I wanted. I was really excited.

So there I sat in math class, with my algebra book in front of me. My teacher was standing at the front of the room. She was explaining the day's assignment. But instead of thinking about algebra, I was planning how I wanted the date to go, starting with asking Jennie out and ending with—getting a good-night kiss? In fact, I spent a lot of the class day-dreaming my way through the whole evening. It would be perfect. First, I would pick her up right on time, and she would be waiting for me, nicely dressed and generally looking great. Then we would go to a little steak house on the east side of town where the food would be affordable but nice. Next, I would try to find out what kind of movies she likes and offer to take her to just that kind. After dinner we would see a movie that she would enjoy. She would whisper to me, "You really know how to pick great movies. I loved it!" Finally, I would drop her off at her house. She would say that she wanted to go out with me again soon.

Just then I felt a tap on my shoulder. Looking up, I saw my teacher standing beside me. Needless to say, I didn't know what we were doing in class. I was still standing on Jennie's front porch, saying good-night; what's more, I was almost ready for that good-night kiss. Naturally, the teacher did not know what a pleasant situation I was in mentally, but she knew how to drag me back to reality. All she had to do was tell me to go up to the board and work problem five. And so that is what I did until the hour was over ten minutes later.

After school that same day, I did ask Jennie for a date, and she said "Yes," to my great relief. But when Saturday night came, nothing went right. When I picked her up, she wasn't ready. The food at the steak house was poor; among other things, the rolls were crunchy, and the meat was rubbery. We tried to carry on a conversation, but we had nothing in common. To make matters worse, we picked a movie that was a real bore, and it felt like it went on for days. By the time I got her back home, I decided it wasn't even worth trying to get a kiss.

All in all, nothing turned out right the whole evening. Later on, I wondered if it ever could have been as great as I imagined. Looking back, I guess it could have been worse; at least I didn't wreck the car.

Exercise 5-4: Analyzing your writing for coherence

DIRECTIONS: *Select any paragraph you wrote earlier in this term, and mark the devices you used to ensure coherence. With your teacher's approval, write in the margins, underline, use circles and arrows, or use any other methods you need to show connections between ideas.*

Compare the frequency and type of your coherence methods with those in the paragraph on coins (page 87). Can you make the links between your ideas clearer? Which method did you use least? Which methods might you use more?

Use the paragraph on stuttering, found just before Practice 5-5 (page 94), as an example.

Exercise 5-5: Analyzing paragraphs in peer groups

DIRECTIONS: *Write a paragraph on a topic of your choice or a topic suggested by your teacher. Bring two copies to class. Before class, on one copy, mark the devices that ensure coherence, following the methods suggested above (see Exercise 5-4).*

Use the unmarked copy for peer work with one other student or for work in groups. During peer evaluation, consider coherence and the devices that are present. Afterward, compare your own assessment of your paper with that of your classmates.

Exercise 5-6: Analyzing an essay for coherence

DIRECTIONS: *Select a paragraph from a magazine article or a nonfiction book. Make two photocopies. On one copy, mark the devices the author used to ensure coherence. Bring both copies to class. Show the unmarked copy to your classmates. You might work in small groups, sharing that copy; or with a projector, you could let the entire class look at the selected paragraph. Then explain your analysis of the paragraph. You may refer to your marked copy as you describe your findings.*

6

Writing Narrative Paragraphs

Understanding Narrative Writing

In the first five chapters, you have read many sample paragraphs. You probably found narratives more interesting than other kinds of writing because narratives tell stories, and readers enjoy stories. Most readers are naturally curious about what happens to other people. Because narratives offer insight into others' lives and experiences, they have great appeal.

The expression "narrative writing" covers an enormous territory. Narratives vary in length from a few sentences to a long novel. Some narratives are based on actual experience. Some are entirely fictitious, and others use a mixture of truth and fiction. Some narratives are meant to amuse; others inform or convey a message to readers. Narratives appear in many forms, including poetry, "regular" prose stories, and drama on the stage, in film, or on television.

In short, you are surrounded by narratives every day, some of them in print, many in the electronic media, and others passed along orally. Historically, folk stories were passed from generation to generation by oral tradition. Good narratives can be spoken just as well as written, but audiences expect more polish and structure in written work.

Because you are well acquainted with narratives, you already have a sense of what works and what doesn't work in narratives. Use Practice 6-1 to recall some stories you liked and others you didn't like.

Practice 6-1.   Remembering narratives

DIRECTIONS: *Answer these questions as you like, expressing your opinions freely. There are no right or wrong answers.*

1. What was the most interesting story you heard (or saw on television) during the past two days? Summarize it in a few words.

   _____

   _____

2. When you heard that story, what specific details caught your interest? (Was it the time or place, the people, the peculiar circumstances, or what?)

   _____

   _____

3. In general, what do you most enjoy about good stories? (Consider the television programs, movies, and novels that you most enjoy.)

   _____

   _____

   _____

4. In general, what don't you like in stories? (Again consider television programs, movies, and novels, as well as other stories.)

   _____

   _____

   _____

   Though answers to Practice 6-1 will vary, you probably will agree that some qualities are found in the narratives you like:

   - They focus on specific persons, places, times, and experiences. They have "characters," "setting," and a situation or problem that makes a "plot."
   - They capture interest by getting readers (viewers) to care about the people caught up in the situation.

- They include the details that are necessary for understanding, but they do not clutter the story with unnecessary details.
- They are easy to follow, and they move fast enough to maintain readers' (viewers') interest.
- They make a point, and that point is clear.

All these qualities are important, and they work together to hold the attention of readers and listeners.

Writers of paragraph-length narratives use their topic sentences to summarize the main points in their stories. Then the other sentences in the paragraph tell the story. If the topic sentences come first in the paragraph, the point may be repeated in a conclusion. This student's paragraph follows that common pattern:

[1]I have never felt such an invasion of privacy as I did the time my car was broken into. [2]I discovered the break-in early one Saturday morning when I was leaving for work. [3]I walked out to my car, which was parked in the street, and got around to the driver's side as usual. [4]Then I noticed the window was broken. [5]It didn't hit me for a couple of seconds that my car had been broken into, but when it did, I was furious. [6]After looking through the car and searching in jacket pockets, I realized my wallet was gone. [7]I had left it in the glove box the night before. [8]In a flash, I thought about the money I had in the wallet, and I knew it amounted to only about four dollars. [9]That was a relief, but only for a split second, because I immediately thought about my credit cards and my driver's license and what a nuisance it would be to report their loss and get replacements. [10]Then I remembered my girlfriend's picture and other pictures. [11]I began to feel sick at the thought of some thief having my personal belongings. [12]But I told myself to calm down and search the house first before getting too panicky. [13]After a quick but thorough search, I called the police. [14]When the police arrived, the officer helped me search the car again. [15]We found some other things missing, but nothing mattered as much as my wallet. [16]The police officer and I got into the police car to file a report. [17]When the incident was over, I realized it could have been worse than it was. [18]Nonetheless, my anger at the invasion of my privacy remains to this day.

Practice 6-2.   Analyzing a student's narrative

DIRECTIONS: *Answer these questions about the paragraph above.*

1. Which is the topic sentence? _____

2. In which sentences does the writer give us the setting (time, place,

   situation)? _____

3. In which sentences does the writer give us evidence to show that his pri-

   vacy was invaded? _____

4. In which sentences does the writer tell us how he felt about the

   situation? _____

5. One sentence could be omitted as not essential to the story. Which one

   is it? _____

6. Underline transitional words and phrases in the paragraph. List three of
   them here, and explain how they connect ideas within the paragraph:

   a. _____

   b. _____

   c. _____

Though narratives often make serious points, many narratives are meant to amuse. Most readers enjoy lighthearted or humorous stories, even if the experiences were not humorous to the people involved at the time. Some readers are also entertained by scary stories, which may be about narrow escapes and other frightening moments in the writers' lives. Such stories may simply thrill readers, or they may be the basis for a serious point. You will read some students' examples in Exercise 6-2 below.

Writers sometimes relate embarrassing moments, not necessarily to convey serious messages, but to amuse and to share those experiences with readers. Here is one example by a student writer:

[1]When I was a teenager working at the county fair, the work crew stopped by the concession stand for a break. [2]After everyone bought

refreshments, our boss drove up in a pickup truck to give us a ride back to the shop. [3]We all jumped into the back of the truck. [4]I was sitting on the open tailgate, eating an ice cream cone. [5]The boss started the truck out very slowly. [6]But when he saw some of his friends walking down the midway, he took off suddenly, forcing two other workers and me to tumble off the tailgate. [7]My ice cream cone went sailing into the air, and I fell to the ground. [8]Luckily only my pride was hurt. [9]As I picked myself off the ground, a crowd of people started laughing at what had just happened. [10]I was so embarrassed and angry that I decided to walk back to the shop before I would ride back with this show-off.

Practice 6-3. Analyzing a student's paragraph

DIRECTIONS: *Answer these questions about the paragraph above.*

1. In your own words, state the topic idea. _____

_____

_____

2. Which sentence comes closest to expressing the topic idea? _____

3. Which sentences provide background information such as time, place,

situation? _____

4. Which details stand out as particularly vivid? _____

_____

_____

Whether narratives convey a serious point or simply entertain, they express main ideas and back them up with supporting information. In other words, narratives follow the main principles of paragraph writing:

- present a topic idea (often in a topic sentence at the beginning)
- support that topic idea with the other sentences

Using Techniques of Narrative Writing

Because narrative writing involves the principles discussed in the preceding chapters, you can think of this study of narrative as a review. In narrative writing you will continue to apply these principles:

1. Select and refine the topic so that a main idea is stated clearly in the topic sentence. In narratives, the main idea will probably deal with conflict or emotional response to conflict.
2. Select appropriate, vivid supporting details. In narratives, the details will tell about time, place, actions, and people's motives and reactions.
3. Organize the information so that readers will be able to understand and follow the story. In narratives, chronological arrangement is normal. Any shifts in time (or place) must be made clear to the reader.

Selecting a Topic

For narratives, as for other kinds of writing, look for possible topics in the places close to you: your background, experiences, interests, and first-hand observations of other people. You will write best when you write about things that really matter to you: personal experiences, beliefs, worries, impressions, and knowledge in specific areas.

Remember that you may begin with many possible topics. Brainstorming will produce related ideas, or sometimes lead you to an even better topic. Before writing, you must examine the possible topics and supporting ideas. The goal is to narrow your focus to a specific instance.

One way to narrow a broad topic is to limit the time and place to a few minutes (or maybe a few hours) and one place. Suppose you enjoy hunting, fishing, and exploring in parks and forests. You are experienced enough to set up camp and live for days in the wilderness. You could tell many stories based on your experiences, but for a brief narrative you would limit yourself to one brief time in one specific place.

In this paragraph, the student writer limited herself to one event:

[1]Although camping is one of my favorite activities, it can be frightening at times. [2]When I was thirteen years old, I went camping with my family in the Carpathian Mountains in Romania. [3]Something terrifying happened to my family and me. [4]The location was one of our favorite campsites, in spite of the many ferocious brown bears in the vicinity. [5]To discourage the bears from visiting us, my mother hid our food in the

trunk of the car, and my father strung battery-powered lights on four wooden poles placed around our tent. [6]About midnight, we put the fire out and crawled into the tent, ready for a good night's sleep. [7]It seemed like only a few minutes later when something struck the tent with enormous force. [8]My eyes popped open, and there on the tent wall was the big, dark shadow of a bear. [9]I was so frightened that I could not make a sound or move. [10]I saw my father motion for silence and closed my eyes to shut out the terrifying sight. [11]Would you believe that I fell asleep? [12]I remember awakening the next morning with a sense that I was lucky to be alive. [13]My father explained that a bear had tripped over one of the anchor ropes and had leaned against the side of the tent. [14]The huge shadow had been created by the safety lights on the poles outside. [15]Explanations did not ease the fear I felt that night, nor has passing time erased that fear from my mind.

Practice 6-4.   Analyzing how a topic is narrowed

DIRECTIONS: *Answer these questions about the paragraph above.*

1. Which is the topic sentence? _____

2. In which sentences does the writer indicate her prior experience with

   camping? _____

3. In which sentences does the writer prepare us for the frightening mo-

   ment she later describes? _____

4. In which sentences does the writer reveal her feelings about this

   episode? _____

5. In your opinion, would the paragraph be better if sentence 11 were a

   statement rather than a question? _____

6. What purposes are served by the last sentence? _____

   _____

As the example above shows, writers who relate personal experiences have specific information to share, not only about the facts, but also about their emotional responses. This example also shows that writers can weave their reactions into the story as they go along. That technique is not necessary, however, and many times writers let readers assume their emotional responses from the facts in the story.

Selecting Details

When you have a workable topic in mind, some details will occur to you immediately, and others will spring to mind as you brainstorm and write your first drafts. You want to select the best details you can. That means selecting relevant, vivid details.

At times you may think of a dramatic moment, full of colorful details sure to grab your readers' attention and hold their interest. If so, writing comes more easily, except that you may not have a main idea until you think about the story later. At times you may be writing simply to share an interesting or amusing experience; your main idea may be implied.

In the next paragraph, a student writer shares a dramatic and amusing moment. Notice the exact information and the well-chosen details:

[1]I am a firefighter with the city fire department. [2]Last fall I responded to a fire call reported by a neighbor as "smoke in the house next door." [3]Upon arrival we donned our self-contained breathing apparatus and entered the house to do a primary search and rescue. [4]We discovered that a meat loaf was burning in the oven, causing the kitchen and much of the house to fill with smoke. [5]I quickly extinguished the meat loaf, then focused on searching for possible victims. [6]I rushed around, hoping I wouldn't find anyone home, but knowing I had to check everywhere to be sure. [7]Upon entering the bathroom, I came upon a lady soaking in the tub. [8]She was listening to loud music and apparently hadn't heard a thing. [9]I guess I must have looked like Darth Vader because she screamed and threw a bottle of shampoo at me. [10]Before entering the bathroom I was worrying about possible victims, but seeing her like that embarrassed me so that I couldn't concentrate on the job I needed to do. [11]Everything worked out well, and it is an experience I will never forget.

Practice 6-5.   Analyzing supporting details

DIRECTIONS: *Answer these questions about the paragraph above.*

1. In which sentences does the writer give us the setting (time, place, situation)? _____

2. List three vivid details that you found in this paragraph.

   a. _____

   b. _____

   c. _____

3. Which sentence comes closest to being a workable topic sentence? _____

4. Suggest a topic idea that would fit this paragraph. You may revise one of the student's sentences or create one of your own. _____

   _____

   _____

5. Suggest a better ending for this story. _____

   _____

   _____

The firefighter chose details that created a clear, exact picture in the reader's mind. You can follow his example: identify objects, their colors, shapes, or sizes. Use specific words, just as he did. For instance, the lady threw "a bottle of shampoo," not "something" or "a nearby object." The smoke came from a meat loaf burning in the oven, not from "something" or "some food on fire."

Besides using details to make the scene vivid, you must provide the details readers need in order to understand the situation. When you write your first draft, you will put in some appropriate details, but you may also end up with some irrelevant ones. Then, as you revise, you must consider which details really matter. You want to include details that help support your main idea.

In this example, a student revised a draft to eliminate irrelevant details and emphasize the relevant ones.

Draft Version

[1]My job is more dangerous than I realized. [2]I worked in construction all summer. [3]By September, I should have known what to expect on a hot day. [4]I was working with cement. [5]It was 94 degrees that day, but we had worked many days in temperatures from 100 to 105 degrees. [6]Cement hardens fast in that kind of heat. [7]I noticed that my legs were itching. [8]But I paid no attention. [9]I just kept working. [10]Wet cement had splattered on my pants, but that was not unusual. [11]That's because wet cement has a tendency to splatter around. [12]Every night I went home with my clothes a complete mess. [13]All of us ran into the same thing every day. [14]We knew we had to scrape the wet cement off fast or ruin our clothes. [15]We also had to watch out for heat stroke in such extreme temperatures. [16]When I finally paid attention that day, I was in such pain that I couldn't go on. [17]I took off my pants and saw large blisters on my knees and thighs. [18]I left the job and drove myself to the hospital. [19]At least I didn't get any cement on the seat of my new car. [20]I was in terrible pain. [21]The doctor treated me for burns and sent me home. [22]She did, however, ask to see me a week later. [23]The burns left me with holes in my pants and a hole in my checkbook because I was out of work for many weeks.

When the writer reconsidered that episode in his life, he realized that the 94-degree heat of the day had been very important. When he revised, he threw out irrelevant details and elaborated on those which mattered.

As you read the revised version of his paragraph, notice how the heat is now shown to be relevant:

[1]Last September 14, I was pouring cement as usual on my construction job. [2]The day was hot for mid-September. [3]It was 94 degrees, miserably hot to work in, but the heat makes cement set quickly. [4]I started to notice that some wet cement was splattering on my pants and soaking through to my skin. [5]I paid no attention until my legs started to itch. [6]Soon they began to hurt, but I ignored the pain and went on working. [7]In a little while the pain was so bad that I couldn't ignore it. [8]Then I took

my pants off and saw large open blisters on my thighs and knees. [9]Horrified at the sight, I drove to the hospital. [10]The pain was getting worse all the time. [11]At the hospital I was treated for first, second, and third-degree burns to my legs. [12]It was a painful way to learn how dangerous my job could be.

Practice 6-6. Contrasting a draft and a finished paragraph

DIRECTIONS: *Contrast the two versions of the paragraph above and answer these questions:*

1. What difference does the 94-degree heat make in this narrative? _____

   _____

2. List two details that the writer threw out of his first draft. Why were those details unimportant or irrelevant?

   One detail: _____

   Reason it was removed: _____

   _____

   Another detail: _____

   Reason it was removed: _____

   _____

3. The writer does not tell us where he was working—on a parking lot or in the basement of a house or elsewhere. Would the paragraph be better if we had that information? Why or why not?

   _____

   _____

4. When the writer cut some of the statements out of the draft, he changed the focus and pace of the story. He created a different effect. Do you agree that he improved the story? Why or why not?

   _____

   _____

   _____

5. If you could talk to the writer of this paragraph, what questions would you ask him about this experience? (In other words, what other details might he have included?)

_____

_____

_____

The goal in selecting details sounds quite simple and obvious: tell the readers what they need to know, nothing more and nothing less. Telling the readers more than they need to know slows them down. Telling them less than they need to know leaves them puzzling over the time, place, or situation. By including enough details, but only appropriate details, you will give readers the information they need.

Organizing the Information

Most of the time, narrative writing is organized chronologically, meaning that events move forward in time. The paragraphs above illustrate that usual progression: the firefighter told of getting the report of a fire, rushing to the location, finding the source of the fire, then searching for victims. The construction worker set the scene, described the first signs of trouble, told about the increasing pain, and finally described the treatment he had.

Sometimes the normal order is changed by using flashbacks. An earlier event is described, disturbing the chronology but providing insight or explanation. Less often, a writer may jump forward in time. You read an example of that kind in Exercise 5-3. The writer's daydreaming took him forward mentally to his Saturday-night date.

Ordinarily, straightforward chronology suits your stories, and it is easy for readers to follow. But if you want to jump back or forward in time, you can, provided you make sure your readers will understand what you are doing. In this student paragraph, the writer is careful to help readers understand the sequence of events, though she does not follow a strict chronology:

[1]Though I'm new at my job with the band, events force me to learn fast. [2]For instance, last Friday night, I had a scare when the stage and the entire dance floor

Sentences 4-12 are a flashback

suddenly went dark. [3]The evening raced through my mind as I tried to think what could have gone wrong. [4]I remembered that we had arrived about six o'clock. [5]The band members had set up first, and then they helped me adjust the speakers and position the lights. [6]We put everything in its place except for the spotlight, but that seemed to be fine right where it was. [7]When the show started at eight, we felt we were ready. [8]The band sounded great. [9]Right away the dance floor filled, and people seemed to be having a good time. [10]I was behind stage adjusting the lights, making sure they flashed and changed colors. [11]After the third song, I hit the spotlight for a guitar solo. [12]Instead of light, everything went pitch black. [13]Fumbling around in the dark, I suddenly realized what had gone wrong. [14]The spotlight had tripped a circuit breaker. [15]That light must have a short. [16]I ran over and unplugged the spotlight, flipped the circuit breakers on, and got everything back to normal. [17]The guitar solo settled everyone down, and we finished the show without problems, but also without that spotlight. [18]Now I know that I have to do more than position the lights; I have to check them in advance.

Here she recalls events earlier in the evening

Sometimes writers organize information so as to build suspense or create a surprise ending. Then information is withheld so that the reader is lured along, picking up clues as in a detective story. At other times the writer gives clues that lead to an amusing ending. In this whimsical paragraph, the early statements entice readers, arouse their curiosity, and keep them reading until they come upon a surprise ending:

> [1]She was standing in the corner, the light reflecting off her soft brown hair. [2]Her eyes were beckoning for attention. [3]As I approached her, a gentleman asked me if I needed some assistance, and so I inquired about her. [4]He said, "She is ten percent off this evening." [5]After asking if she was clean and in good health and being assured she was, I walked over to her. [6]I held her in my arms, and she gave me a kiss. [7]She looked longingly into my eyes, and I caressed her face. [8]I asked how much she would cost, and the man said, "Fifty-five dollars." [9]I paid at once and took the cuddly rabbit home. [10]Rabbits are lovable and inexpensive pets.

Practice 6-7.   Considering titles

DIRECTIONS: *Because paragraphs are short, they don't usually need titles, but the student who wrote this paragraph decided to use a title. He wrote "How Clean Are Your Thoughts?" for his title. Think a bit about titles, and answer these opinion questions.*

1. As a reader, would you find the paragraph above more enjoyable with

   the title printed at the top? _____

   _____

2. What purposes do titles serve? _____

   _____

   _____

3. Besides brevity, what are the qualities of a good title? _____

   _____

   _____

   _____

4. As a reader, what connections might you see between a well-chosen title and the body of the paragraph (or other piece of writing)? _____

_____

_____

5. Suggest a possible title for the paragraph above about the firefighter who extinguished a burning meat loaf. _____

_____

Writers can use narratives for their own sake or as part of other kinds of writing. Narratives are among the most enjoyable kinds of reading for readers and writing for writers. The principles are more or less self-evident: select a narrow enough topic, select appropriate details, and organize so that the reader can follow the sequence of events.

Summary

- The term "narrative" means storytelling.
- Narratives are of all lengths and many forms.
- Good narratives are clear and well focused; they move fast enough to hold the interest of the audience.
- Good narratives provide the necessary details to make the story understandable.
- Good narratives make a point.
- Narratives can be serious or lighthearted; they can be used for their own sake or as part of other pieces of writing.
- Writing a narrative paragraph requires these steps:
  —selecting and refining a topic;
  —selecting relevant, vivid details;
  —organizing the statements.
- Most narratives are organized chronologically.

Exercise 6-1:   Organizing ideas into a paragraph

DIRECTIONS: *These two sets of statements were produced by brainstorming. The students had narrowed their topics, then began brainstorming to develop ideas for paragraphs.*

Select one set of statements and create a paragraph based upon them. Invent other details, if you like, and rewrite any of these statements to suit your paragraph. You do not have to use every item given below. In class, discuss your version along with those of your classmates.

Set 1

Awoke to another Monday morning, ugh. Came too soon.

Have to leave early and drive, then park and get to the office by 8:00 A.M.

Washed my face, put on makeup, waiting for coffee to brew.

Hurried to get dressed. Seemed like I was running late and couldn't catch up.

Day was routine. Lots of phone calls and customers.

Felt I was forgetting something. Even before I left my apartment.

Couldn't figure out what I forgot.

No one at work said anything out of the ordinary to me.

Finally time to drive home.

Lots of traffic, many stops in the congestion.

Glanced at my face in the rear-view mirror.

No particular reason to look in the mirror, just killing time in the slow traffic.

Couldn't believe my eyes.

Saw eye makeup on one eye and not on the other.

Set 2

Just a high-school freshman.

Very self-conscious, early adolescence.

Never forget the first day of that school, a total disaster.

Woke up late. Startled. Looked at the clock in astonishment.

Didn't want to look like a dumb freshman.

Wanted to act like I knew my way around.

Wanted to get to school early and find the classrooms.

Ended up late for first class.

Took ten minutes to find the room.

Felt my heart pound as I ran down the hall looking for the right room.

Walked in and looked for a chair.

No empty chairs.

Felt like an idiot.

Teacher stopped, tried to find another chair.

Found one, then I sat for a moment.

Had to leave.

Felt really stupid.

Said something like, "Sorry. I think I'm in the wrong room."

Room full of seniors.

Exercise 6-2: Revising paragraphs

DIRECTIONS: *Students wrote these narratives. To make the paragraphs stronger, revise them by rewording sentences and changing any details you like. You may add or subtract information. You may invent additional details, if you like. You may rearrange the order, change the ending, and make any other changes you wish.*

Revise between the lines and in the margins. Then create a clean copy to bring to class. Compare your versions with those of your classmates.

Paragraph 1

One night I went in to work. I worked at a small neighborhood deli as a cashier. One of the other girls asked me to come in and close for her. She had a date and wanted to leave early. After I had been there for about fifteen minutes, two men approached the register. This was a little odd because in this deli customers paid the waitresses for their meal tickets. The men had been having dessert. I didn't pay too much attention to them. I just rang up their check and asked them for the amount of money. That's when one of the men told me to give him all the money in the register. I looked at him in amazement and asked him if he was kidding. That's when I saw the gun they were holding. I was in complete shock. I immediately pulled all the cash from the register and handed it over. Then they were gone. This all happened so fast that I barely had time to think. It was amazing to me that out of about ten people in the room including my boyfriend, no one noticed this happening. I was just glad that no one was hurt.

Paragraph 2

I was traveling on Highway 7, just west of the interstate. The car ahead of me passed a truck in the right lane, and so did I. Then I pulled my cycle up beside that car. Without warning it swerved right at me! I slammed on my brakes, but it kept coming faster. Then it was pulling past me, missing me by a couple of inches. That's what I hoped. Boom! The bumper had hit my front tire. It took my motorcycle out from under me. All I could do was watch the pavement get closer and closer. I felt myself sliding along the roadway. I felt a burning sensation in my leg, and it started to hurt something awful. I closed my eyes and stretched out so I could roll. My eighteen years of life passed before my eyes twice. Once I saw a hubcap from the car, rolling backward. It was an odd sight. I put my arm out to get up, and I was shot through the air like out of a slingshot, three times. Finally I stopped rolling. I got up and looked for the things I had lost in the spill. I found my shades, wallet, and left shoe along the side of the road. I could not see my bike on the road, so I hopped into the ditch to find it. It was all smashed up. I found it in a thicket of weeds. I lifted it upright and pulled the key from the ignition. Even that was all bent up! Then I climbed back up to the roadway. I stood there on the shoulder of the road and watched the same officer who had given me a ticket the week before drive up. Later I learned that this whole thing happened because the people in the car wanted to throw a beer bottle at a road sign.

Exercise 6-3:   Completing narratives

DIRECTIONS: *Choose **any one** of the passages below, and add a paragraph or more to end the story. Invent any details you like. You may change these openings somewhat, if your story needs slightly different details at the start. Compare your stories with those of your classmates.*

Passage 1

I guess there's one of me in every pool hall. I'm what you'd call a hustler, a shark, a big-money guy. But I'm the best—or at least undefeated—in the games that count. I'm such a dude to some kid who thinks he's so hot as he walks in. They're all the same. I buy him a can of pop, have him play on my table, lose some close games, and make him think he's so hot. Then I play him for a couple of friendly bucks, and sure enough, I lose some more close games. Then I nail him.

Passage 2

She woke up the way she always woke up. Her favorite doll was on her window by her bed, staring at her with that Hollywood-glamorous smile, which to her was just the world's way of saying, "Good Morning, Shelly. Did you have a nice sleep?" She did. "Good morning, Barbie," she said.

She turned over to her left and saw the clock on her dresser. It was almost ten o'clock. All her friends were in Mrs. DeRocher's second-grade class by now, even that rat fink Freddie who poured sand in her friend Katie's hair. Shelly felt fine, but the city council still wouldn't let her go to school, not with AIDS, they wouldn't.

Passage 3

The party was nicely under way. Friends and neighbors were visiting, telling jokes, and bragging about their kids, as parents do. When the phone rang, I was called to talk to Jacob, my eleven-year-old son. He told me he wanted to ride his bike to a convenience store and rent a movie. I said it was okay. I also said that Jeff, his younger brother, could go along, and they should carry flashlights because it was getting dark.

When I hung up, I didn't think I had anything to worry about. The store was only a mile from the house, and there wasn't much traffic in this small town. But within a half hour, I was again called to the phone. This time it was Jeff, and he was crying so hard I couldn't make out much except "Someone took Jacob!" Gradually I began to get the story. "A man with a mask pulled a gun on us and made us lie in a ditch. He told me to run away, so I did. When I looked back, the man was gone, and so was Jacob."

Passage 4

My flight home started uneventfully, but about an hour after we took off, the captain announced that we had to make an emergency landing. He explained that the landing-gear indicator light was malfunctioning. Those words didn't mean much to me, but I was glad that he sounded very calm all the while. I noticed that the man beside me turned pale and gripped the armrest until his knuckles were white. I could not help thinking about the recent crash of a DC-10 in Iowa, and I suppose that crash was on his mind, too. Then the pilot spoke again, saying that he would have to jettison a lot of the plane's fuel.

Right after the captain made his first announcement, the flight attendants began to reassure the passengers. They coached us on placing our heads between our knees, a position I recognized as the crash-preparation position described on the emergency instructions card. I tried to listen and follow every detail, but panic was getting in the way. Was I about to die?

Passage 5

It was a warm summer day, about 85 degrees. I was sitting around the house, bored and wondering what to do. Nothing seemed promising there, so I went out to the garage. Right then, I noticed my father's toolbox with all those intriguing tools, like a hammer, nails, screwdrivers, and a wrench. Nearby he had a couple of saws and clamps, lots of things a boy could play with. Next I went out to the back yard to see what I might do there. The first thing I saw was a pile of wood, almost enough to build a fort. That idea faded for a moment, but then I noticed the neighbors' big trees. Bingo! What a fabulous idea. We'll make a tree fort.

When you're ten years old, little harebrained notions can get out of hand in a hurry. I called my buddy Eric, and he came over right away. Usually Eric and I didn't do things that would get us into trouble. This day was different. We got started right away. We picked out the biggest tree in the neighbors' yard and climbed almost to the top, carrying my dad's saws with us.

Exercise 6-4: Analyzing narrative writing

DIRECTIONS: *Watch for narrative paragraphs in newspaper or magazine articles. Writers often begin or end with short anecdotes. Find a good example of narrative writing. Bring the article or a photocopy and compare your example with those of your classmates.*

Analyze the elements of narrative writing in the article, applying the concepts included in this chapter. Then consider how the narrative fits into the article overall.

Exercise 6-5: Writing a narrative

DIRECTIONS: *Write a narrative in one or more paragraphs. If you use more than one paragraph, make sure each one is well developed and supports your main point.*

Suggestions: Use a moment of fear, anxiety, embarrassment, awe, joy, sorrow, or other strong emotion. Think about what happened, how you got into the situation and out of it. Focus on yourself primarily, not others. Generally, the more emotionally charged and dramatic an experience is at the time, the better story it makes afterward. You can more easily (and more dramatically) tell about a car accident than about a birthday party.

Use an episode that took place in a few minutes or a few seconds, not days or weeks. You can make a better story out of the panic of losing your wallet or getting stuck in an elevator than you can out of the first three weeks on a new job.

Bring your papers to class for peer evaluation.

7

Writing Descriptive Paragraphs

Looking at Descriptive Paragraphs

Descriptive writing has one main purpose: to give readers a vivid mental picture of something the writer has seen, heard, or felt. Writers create an explicit picture in readers' minds by offering some details rather than others and by emphasizing some features more than others.

Good descriptive writing meets these standards:

- It creates a clear, definite picture in the reader's mind.
- It offers enough well-chosen detail so that the reader can understand, even if the subject is complicated or unfamiliar.
- It *shows* the reader what is meant; it does not merely *tell* the reader.
- It is organized so that the reader can form an accurate mental picture.
- It uses specific, vivid details, appealing to the reader's senses.

To create a clear mental picture for readers, you must focus on one main idea so that your readers get one clear, main impression. Achieving this goal takes close observation and concentration. Those who write a series of vague, general statements give only a hazy notion about their main points. Those who string random bits of detail together into paragraphs only confuse and bore readers. Rather, you want to select details well and focus on one clear picture.

That one clear picture is sometimes called a "**main impression**" or a "**dominant impression.**" The main or dominant impression is the specific, limited view or interpretation that you want to convey about your topic. That impression is stated in your topic sentence; it is your controlling idea.

In these paragraphs, the students gave their readers clear main impressions. One writer describes a lake; the other describes a Mexican ghetto. Many views and interpretations are possible within these topics. But, as you will see, these writers convey specific main impressions; their interpretations of a lake and a ghetto are distinct and evident, beginning with the opening statements. Notice that all the details in the paragraphs support the controlling ideas found in the topic sentences:

Paragraph A

[1]When I spend time at the lake, I have peace of mind unlike that I find anywhere else. [2]The beautiful, unpolluted water seems to stare back at me when I look into it. [3]The purity of the water reminds me of a child's blue eyes. [4]Innocence and tranquillity come to mind as I look across the lake to the silent woods beyond. [5]I know that the lake is not entirely quiet because it is home to many fish and birds, including good-sized bass that come up to feed early in the morning. [6]A few times I have sat, half asleep, on the crudely constructed dock that stretches out into the water. [7]Though some of its slats are waterlogged, the dock is firmly secured to the lake bottom by concrete blocks, so that it makes an adequate fishing platform. [8]On many summer days I have been there, holding a fishing line in my hand, but whether I catch anything or not, I enjoy basking in the serenity of my surroundings.

Paragraph B

[1]I saw much evidence of extreme poverty in a Mexican ghetto. [2]People lived in houses amounting to nothing but tiny shacks with windows. [3]These shacks were made of dry, splintered wood with paint peeling away. [4]When they had yards, they were tiny patches of bare earth with a few long, scraggly weeds. [5]Some of these shacks had fences made from concrete slabs, sometimes with jagged pieces of glass protruding from the slabs. [6]The people wore dirty clothing, most of it tattered beyond repair, and most of the children had no shoes. [7]But perhaps worst of all, the streets were littered with rubbish and garbage. [8]No one seemed to care about the prospect of disease, and no one seemed to notice the stench. [9]As a visitor, I noticed, and I will never forget what I saw.

Practice 7-1.   **Finding dominant impressions**

DIRECTIONS: *Answer these questions about the paragraphs above:*

1. What is the dominant impression you get from Paragraph A?

   _____

   _____

2. Name two details that help create that impression.

   a. _____

   b. _____

3. What is the dominant impression you get from Paragraph B?

   _____

   _____

4. Name two details that help create that impression.

   a. _____

   b. _____

   The paragraphs just before Practice 7-1, like other descriptive passages, could serve many purposes. They can be enjoyed in their own right as passages that appeal to the senses and create mental images. But they could also fit into other kinds of writing, serving purposes beyond simple enjoyment. They might set a scene or evoke a mood within a narrative. Or they might explain and inform readers, many of whom could not vacation at a lake or visit Mexico except in their imagination.

   You will need to describe in greater detail when your topics are unfamiliar or complex. At such times your readers need a lot of help in forming mental pictures. If you describe well, your readers will be able to visualize things that they have never seen or experienced.

   For instance, the three paragraphs below help readers visualize the pyramids of ancient Egypt. Few readers have visited the Middle East, so they could not have walked into these tombs. Even so, readers can picture the scene mentally because of the clear, detailed description this writer provides:

.These beautifully-sculptured scenes impress every visitor to Egypt. Weary with walking over sand and rock in the hot sun, he enters the cool depths of a tomb, and there, on the walls, the ancient peoples come suddenly and startlingly to life. Here is the official himself, the "Chief Scribe to His Majesty" or the "Vizier" (prime minister of the king) wearing a white kilt of linen and seated on a chair of office, watching ranks of his servants bringing offerings of meat, bread, beer and wine. Here men are netting wildfowl in the marshes beside the Nile. There others are spearing fish, or plucking fowl. Women-servants are reaping the crops, or grinding corn in stone querns. Butchers are carving up the carcasses of cattle, while others carry the severed haunches to their master. Nearby a man drives a group of asses bearing loads. But the sculptor, tiring of the conventional scenes which he has to depict in every tomb, has introduced, as artists will, a note of variety. One of the asses is giving trouble; and two men are wrestling with the stubborn little beast, in whose eyes is a devilish glint. One grasps his foreleg; the other hauls at his bridle. For one moment the humorous observation of an individual who died fifty centuries ago reaches us, and we smile with him.

We look upwards, and there is yet another scene; the elegant wife of the official, her slender body clothed in a close-fitting robe of fine, transparent linen, and wearing rich jewelry on her arms and neck, presides with her husband over a party; her guests sit on chairs or recline on cushions, served with wine and delicacies by naked slave girls. A group of musicians plays for the guests, and a girl dancer sways her hips to the rhythmic clapping of hands, the tapping of tambourines and the strumming of lutes. In one corner a rank of chorus girls is executing a concerted high kick of which the New York "Rockettes" would not be ashamed. One can see such a scene in the tomb of Mahu at Sakkara, and at other places.

Let your eye wander further along the wall, and you are enjoying a day's sport in the marshes, with the official, his wife and daughter. A light skiff made of bound papyrus stems glides beside the reeds. Beaters have roused the wildfowl, which circle over our heads; the official, owner of the tomb, sends his throwing stick whirling among them, while his daughter clings to his legs to prevent his falling into the water. His wife holds a duck in her hand, while servants go to gather the fallen birds. All these scenes are carefully described in hieroglyphic texts above or below the sculptured reliefs.

Here, before our eyes, is a sophisticated people who enjoyed sport, who understood the art of dress, music, and civilized entertainment, who valued fine cooking and good wines, who, without doubt, also had a literature. . . .

—From Leonard Cottrell, *The Anvil of Civilization* (New York: Mentor Books, 1957), 75–76.

Practice 7-2. Finding details explaining the unfamiliar

DIRECTIONS: *Answer these questions about the paragraphs above:*

1. Name three specific details that stand out as particularly vivid in the first paragraph.

   a. _____

   b. _____

   c. _____

2. Name three specific details that stand out as particularly vivid in the second paragraph.

   a. _____

   b. _____

   c. _____

3. Name three specific details that stand out as particularly vivid in the third paragraph.

   a. _____

   b. _____

   c. _____

4. Which details lead us to agree with the author's view of the ancient people as "a sophisticated people . . . who understood the art of dress, music, and civilized entertainment"? Add two specific details to this list.

   a. At the dinner party, guests were entertained with music and dancing, "the tapping of tambourines and the strumming of lutes." This scene supports the idea that the people understood "the art of music and civilized entertainment."

   b. _____

   _____

   _____

   c. _____

   _____

   _____

5. What is the main idea in each paragraph?

   a. First paragraph _____

   b. Second paragraph _____

   c. Third paragraph _____

As you see in the example above, it takes more details and, consequently, more words, to **show** than to **tell**. To show that the ancient Egyptians were a sophisticated people who understood (among other things) "the art of dress, music, and civilized entertainment," the author used many exact details. Because the culture is totally unfamiliar to most readers, many details are essential if readers are to form a clear mental picture.

Choosing and Organizing Details

Good descriptive writing **shows rather than tells.** Showing requires more details than telling, as you see here:

Telling

> Paul was sleepy this morning.

Showing

> Paul yawned, nodded his head, and rubbed his eyes. When I asked him a question in class, he did not answer me. I saw his eyes close for a few seconds, but he looked up again momentarily, as if he wanted to pay attention. Then, almost at once, he nodded, and his eyes closed again.

Often you use the topic sentence to tell the reader, and the supporting sentences to show the reader. This arrangement of ideas is called **deductive**, meaning that you begin with a fairly general statement, then add specific support. The next example uses a deductive arrangement. Notice that the topic sentence is first; it is underlined. The writer tells, then shows:

> <u>Paul was sleepy this morning.</u> He yawned, nodded his head, and rubbed his eyes. When I asked him a question in class, he did not answer me. I saw his eyes close for a few seconds, but he looked up again momentarily, as if he wanted to pay attention. Then, almost at once, he nodded, and his eyes closed again.

The opposite arrangement, called **inductive**, gives specific statements first, leading to the general statement at the end. The general statement states the dominant impression that has been conveyed by the details in the paragraph.

The example below uses the same material and expresses the same dominant impression as the one above: Paul is sleepy this morning. But in this paragraph, first the writer shows (uses details), then tells (gives the generalization). Therefore, as you see, the supporting statements come first; the paragraph ends with the topic sentence:

> Paul yawned, nodded his head, and rubbed his eyes. When I asked him a question in class, he did not answer me. I saw his eyes close for a few seconds, but he looked up again momentarily, as if he wanted to pay attention. Then, almost at once, he nodded, and his eyes closed again. <u>Paul was sleepy this morning.</u>

If the writer merely states, "Paul was sleepy this morning," readers will ask, "How do you know?" Readers need to be shown, not merely told. A flat statement of fact—even a simple fact such as "Paul was sleepy this morning"—does not create a mental picture for readers, nor does it convince readers. Writers must *show* rather than tell to answer readers' questions and create mental pictures.

To create those clear mental pictures for your readers, answer that typical question, "How do you know?" Your answer will usually be based on what you have seen, heard, or otherwise perceived through the senses. You will follow the example shown in the paragraphs above. There the writer used observations to conclude that Paul was sleepy. The question "How do you know?" was answered by first-hand observations. The writer had seen Paul yawning and nodding and got no answer when speaking to Paul.

Practice 7-3.   Creating details to support a dominant impression

DIRECTIONS: *First, invent three details that will show the reader what is meant by each of the generalizations below.*

Second, select any one of these problems and create a paragraph using these details and others that come to mind as you write. Experiment with deductive and inductive patterns. Write on separate paper.

1. Megan's car is damaged beyond repair. (Ask yourself, "What does it look like?")

    a. _____

    b. _____

    c. _____

2. Carla's jacket is nicely designed. (Again, "What does it look like?")

    a. _____

    b. _____

    c. _____

3. The background noise at XYZ's Restaurant is so distracting that I don't enjoy eating there. (Ask yourself, "What noises do I hear?")

    a. _____

    b. _____

    c. _____

4. That lady's face shows that she had a hard life. (Ask yourself, "What do I see that suggests stress, anxiety, illness, or hardship?")

   a. _____

   b. _____

   c. _____

5. The holiday meal was not only festive, but delicious. (Ask yourself, "What did I see, smell, and taste?)

   a. _____

   b. _____

   c. _____

To create vivid impressions, you can draw upon all five senses: seeing, hearing, tasting, touching, and feeling. Of course, you might not use all these in every description, but you can often use several of them, even when describing a simple, common object.

One way to find appropriate details has already been discussed, then tried, in Practice 7-3. There you asked questions that the reader might ask, such as "What did you see? What does it look like? What did you hear?" Another way to discover details is to observe carefully and record impressions as they come along. Later, select the most relevant and vivid of those impressions for your writing.

In Exercise 7-1, you will have a chance to see how well this strategy works for you. The student who wrote the paragraph below began with the lists you see at the opening of that exercise. After several attempts and some hard work in revising, the student wrote this paragraph:

[1]My first cup of coffee warms and stimulates me on these cold school mornings. [2]As it brews, I am tantalized by the rich aroma. [3]That pungent aroma helps me clear the sleepiness from my mind, and it prompts me to get going. [4]When I am dressed, I relax a few minutes over my steaming cup of coffee. [5]Because it is so hot, I am forced to slow down and wait while it cools enough so that I can drink it. [6]Meanwhile, I enjoy the gentle sounds of the spoon hitting the cup as I stir in the cream. [7]Still half asleep, I watch as if in a trance while the deep brown turns into a soft beige. [8]The colors are soothing, though not as soothing as the gentle warm liquid that I sip ever so slowly. [9]I have to be careful that I don't get burned. [10]The slightly bitter taste of the coffee convinces me that I am

really awake and about to face another day. [11]When the caffeine starts to take effect, my sluggish body really comes to life. [12]Soon I am ready to face the world with energy and with enthusiasm, thanks to my early morning coffee.

Practice 7-4.   Analyzing a descriptive paragraph

DIRECTIONS: *Answer these questions about the paragraph above.*

1. Which sentences provide details pertaining to sight? _____

_____

2. Which sentences provide details pertaining to hearing? _____

_____

3. Which sentences provide details pertaining to taste? _____

_____

4. Which sentences provide details pertaining to feeling? _____

_____

5. Which is the topic sentence? _____

6. Is the paragraph deductive or inductive? _____

    How do you know? _____

_____

7. Which impressions did the student leave out when writing the paragraph? (See the lists in Exercise 7-1, pages 143–144.)

_____

_____

    After you have specific, appropriate details, you need to organize them so that the reader can follow your thoughts. Descriptive writing can be arranged in general-to-specific (deductive) or specific-to-general (inductive) patterns. As you saw above, in paragraphs about Paul's sleepiness, both deductive and inductive arrangements worked well.

If you look at those paragraphs again, you will see that the first details about Paul are the first and most noticeable signs of his sleepiness: he yawns, nods, and rubs his eyes. The next statement tells what happened after the yawning, nodding, and rubbing of his eyes: he did not hear a question addressed to him. A time sequence is suggested even though the sequence is not strictly chronological.

In some situations, you can organize according to a **spatial** arrangement. The word "spatial" is derived from the word "space." In a spatial arrangement, you will guide your readers from one point to another. Many directions are possible, such as from wall to floor, object to object, person to person, left to right, top to bottom, clockwise, or the reverse of these. The point is that the mind's eye will be guided in a logical way.

To describe a room, you might begin with an eye-appealing feature, then move toward the right around the room. Here a writer describes her impressions of a living room:

> The living room makes me think of a library because it is quiet, neutral in its color scheme, and has books everywhere I look. As I walk into the room, three large bookcases immediately catch my eye. They are about seven feet tall, and together they extend across the entire south wall. Glancing past the books, figurines, and small plants on the shelves, I notice that to the right of the bookcases, a large fern soaks in the sunshine from the west windows. Unlike a library, however, the windows are set about eighteen inches out from the wall. Though they aren't bay windows, their placement creates somewhat the same spacious effect. Softly patterned, ceiling-to-floor drapes are pulled back, allowing me to see a young maple tree on the front lawn. A long beige couch stretches across in front of the windows, and in front of the couch is a pentagon-shaped, glass-topped coffee table. I notice large picture books on the coffee table, as if inviting me to sit and browse. Opposite the long couch, a desk waits quietly for a writer.

On second thought, this writer realized that the entire room was too much to describe in one paragraph. She cut back the material so that she could focus on the wall units mentioned at the start of the paragraph above:

> Large walnut bookcases with books, planters, and small figurines catch the eye. These bookcases are taller than I am, and they extend

across the entire south wall. Though the books and other objects are nicely arranged, I am first struck by the beauty of the bookcases them-selves. The wood is a deep, rich brown, with a slight gloss and only a touch of ornate carving. The center unit has glass doors on the upper half, and over the glass, pencil-slim strips of wood cross to form long diamond shapes that draw the eye upward. Looking closely, I see that the lower parts of the bookcases have drawers or storage compartments.

The less territory a writer tries to cover, the more detailed the para-graph can be. The more detailed the paragraph is, the clearer the picture in the reader's mind.

Practice 7-5.   Selecting details for a descriptive paragraph

DIRECTIONS: *Consider your living room or another room that you see daily. What details would you use to describe that room for someone who has never seen it? First, you need to consider these questions:*

1. What part of the room draws the immediate attention of anyone who walks into the room? (Typical possibilities include a large or unusual piece of furniture, windows and perhaps the view outside, a fireplace, and a painting or other wall decoration.)

   _____

   _____

2. Beginning with a part of the room, you would move through space with the description. In which direction would you move? Right, left, ceiling to floor, or some other?

   _____

   _____

3. List five items that you would include in the one-paragraph description of the room. Put them in the order you chose in answering question 2.

   a. _____

   b. _____

   c. _____

d. _____

e. _____

4. Suppose that you were writing a descriptive paragraph limited to the part of the room you mentioned in answering question 1 above. List five items that you would include in that paragraph.

a. _____

b. _____

c. _____

d. _____

e. _____

Practice 7-6. Writing a descriptive paragraph

DIRECTIONS: *On separate paper, create a paragraph using the material you created in Practice 7-5.*

As a writer, you will sometimes describe an object to make a point about yourself, not about the object. In paragraphs A and B below, the student writers tell about themselves while focusing on objects.

Sometimes readers do not need much description of the object because it is well known, but the point being made about the object takes explaining. For example, when writing Paragraph A, the student realized that readers know what softballs look like, so she did not have to get into the size, shape, or construction of a softball. Instead, she describes the significance of a specific softball.

Paragraph A

[1]One thing that means a great deal to me is the softball that I have displayed in my room. [2]It is the ball I hit for my only home run during my three years of high-school softball. [3]On it I have written the words "home run" and "May 13, 1990," the date I hit it. [4]Whenever I go into my room and look at it, great memories of that game come back to me. [5]I will never forget the super feeling of circling the bases. [6]That ball is also a

reminder of those special days during April and May of my senior year. [7]My teammates and I had finished with twenty wins and three losses before going to the first round of the state tournament. [8]I believe having this particular softball will always be a quiet reminder of our accomplishments together. [9]Still, most of all, hitting that home run was one of the greatest feelings I've ever had, and I'll never forget it, especially with that softball in my room to remind me.

By contrast, the student who wrote Paragraph B needed to describe both the object—her A.A. medallion—and its significance. Because many readers would not know what the medallion looks like, this writer helps readers by giving details that create a mental picture.

Paragraph B

[1]My A.A. (Alcoholics Anonymous) medallion has a very special meaning for me. [2]A.A. gives its members medallions at three months, then again at six months, nine months, one year, eighteen months, and two years. [3]After two years, members get medallions annually. [4]When I look at mine, I see that it looks like a round coin with writing on both sides. [5]On the back is the serenity prayer that all members know by heart. [6]On the front is a triangle with a word on each side: on the left "unity," on the right "service," and on the bottom, "recovery." [7]Across the top is "To thine own self be true." [8]All these words have meaning, but most of all, inscribed within the triangle is the length of time I have been sober, eighteen months now. [9]Those are the words that mean the most to me. [10]I cannot help thinking back to the time before A.A., and terrible memories come to mind. [11]Sometimes now as I hold my medallion, without thinking, I rub my fingers across it, as if to rub out the bitter memories. [12]Without a doubt, the reason my medallion is so special is that I earned it by staying sober, and because of that achievement, I am proud of myself.

Practice 7-7. Analyzing descriptive paragraphs

DIRECTIONS: *Answer these questions about Paragraphs A and B above.*

1. What is the topic idea in Paragraph A?

   _____

   _____

2. Which details support that topic idea?

   _____

   _____

   _____

3. What is the topic idea in Paragraph B?

   _____

   _____

4. Which details support the writer's assertion that the medallion means a lot to her?

   _____

   _____

   _____

5. Would quoting the serenity prayer immediately after sentence 5 improve Paragraph B? Why or why not? (Assume that quoting the prayer would add two or three sentences to the paragraph.)

   _____

   _____

   _____

6. Which has stronger support for its topic idea, Paragraph A or B? _____

   Why do you think so? _____

   _____

   _____

Besides writing about objects, you will also have occasion to describe people. You might focus on their physical descriptions or their personalities or both. In the paragraph below, a student writer limits her description to one personality trait of her friend, namely, Arlette's fear of cats. Notice that specific examples illustrate Arlette's reactions. Readers are prepared for the dominant impression found in a topic sentence at the end:

> As a three-year-old child, my friend Arlette was frightened by an angry, hissing cat. The animal did her no harm, but to this day she is terrified of cats. She runs away from them. She will even run away from cute little kittens tumbling about the floor in play. Arlette tries hard to control her reactions. When she comes to visit me, she tells me I can leave my cat in the room with us. Even so, I keep a watchful eye on him. Usually he settles himself in a warm spot and dozes while we drink coffee and talk. Sometimes his natural curiosity prompts him to approach her and brush lightly against her leg. I can see that Arlette wants to stay calm, and she tries. But I realize that a chill runs through her body, so I pick up the cat and take him away. As a friend, I have learned to live with her fear. She can't seem to overcome it, and she probably won't outgrow it. Apparently Arlette will have a lifelong fear of cats.

As you have seen, descriptive writing is valuable in many situations, and it is pleasing because it appeals to the senses. Because it can create mental pictures, it helps readers visualize people, places, and things they will never see in reality. Description is also a useful part of narratives and other kinds of writing.

Depending on the complexity of the topic and your readers' prior understanding, you might describe it in a few sentences or in many paragraphs. In descriptive writing, you often organize spatially, but you can select any logical order that will help readers.

Summary

- The purpose of descriptive writing is to create a picture in the reader's mind.

- A descriptive paragraph conveys a main or dominant impression of the subject. That impression is often the controlling idea within the topic sentence.

- Generally, the less the reader knows about the topic, the more details the writer must provide. To create a clear mental picture for readers, you must select details that support the dominant impression.

- You need to show, not just tell, the reader. To show the reader, use specific details.

- In a deductive arrangement of ideas, the general statement is first, and supporting details follow. This arrangement can be called the general-to-specific pattern.

- In an inductive arrangement of ideas, the supporting details are first, and the general statement is last. This arrangement can be called the specific-to-general pattern.

- Another way to organize descriptive writing is by a spatial arrangement, that is, by moving through space to guide the reader.

- The less territory writers try to cover, the more detailed the description can be.

Exercise 7-1: Recording impressions

DIRECTIONS: *Pick any hour or two during the next week. If you wish, select a special time, such as a family dinner or an evening at the amusement park. Or, if you like, use an ordinary time, such as the time you spend commuting to or from work or school.*

Carefully observe what is going on around you, and observe your feelings. Then record your impressions on the "sense chart" below. When your chart is complete, look for a main idea in your listings. On separate paper, create a descriptive paragraph on that idea, using selected details from your chart as support.

Example

Sense Chart

(used by the student who wrote the paragraph about coffee,
pages 135–136 above)

Time, place:	early morning, a school day, my apartment
What I saw:	alarm clock—6:30
	light coming in under window shade
	coffee pot on the stove
	coffee steaming in my cup, cream pouring
	brown coffee turning yellowish with cream
What I heard:	alarm clock ringing
	radio news, weather forecast

coffee perking
sound of the spoon against coffee cup
What I smelled, tasted: coffee aroma
bitter taste, but soothing, warm
toast in toaster, then dry and
warm, crumbly, no butter
How I felt: sleepy, don't want to get up
jarred by sound of radio
awakened by the caffeine, get some energy

Sense Chart

Time, place: _____

What I saw: _____

_____

_____

_____

What I heard: _____

_____

_____

_____

What I smelled, tasted, touched: _____

_____

_____

_____

How I felt: _____

_____

_____

_____

Exercise 7-2:   Revising topic sentences for descriptive paragraphs

DIRECTIONS: *College students wrote the sentences below as topic sentences for descriptive paragraphs. Revise these topic sentences so that the controlling ideas will convey clear main impressions. Add details as you like.*

Example: My roommate is good looking.
My roommate Molly is striking and photogenic.

1. The shopping mall was busy.

   _____

   _____

2. After I had been on campus a while, I realized that the library was the best place to study.

   _____

   _____

3. My boss has a strange personality.

   _____

   _____

4. Watching the sun rise over the ocean was a good experience.

   _____

   _____

5. The hotel obviously deserved the rating given in the tour book.

   _____

   _____

6. That cereal ad certainly got my attention.

   _____

   _____

7. The quilt my grandmother made is lovely.

_____

_____

8. Last year's Christmas stamp was one of the most beautiful I have seen, and as a stamp collector, I should know.

_____

_____

9. That crisp October morning was ideal for hunting.

_____

_____

10. The restaurant was festive because of the seasonal decorations.

_____

_____

Exercise 7-3:   Adding details to support topic ideas

DIRECTIONS: *List three descriptive details that would support these general statements.*

Example: That china teapot brings back memories of my grandmother.

a. I saw her handle that teapot with great care when she washed and dried it.
b. She kept it on her kitchen counter all the time.
c. We always had tea when we visited her.

1. That billboard caught my attention right away.

a. _____

b. _____

c. _____

2. The oil spill created a big mess all around the harbor.

   a. _____

   b. _____

   c. _____

3. I rejoice to see the first signs of spring.

   a. _____

   b. _____

   c. _____

4. The shopping mall was busy that morning.

   a. _____

   b. _____

   c. _____

5. It is delightful to walk into the kitchen just as the bread comes out of the oven.

   a. _____

   b. _____

   c. _____

6. I look forward to the carnival atmosphere at the state fair.

   a. _____

   b. _____

   c. _____

7. Watching the fans can be as much fun as watching the football game.

   a. _____

   b. _____

   c. _____

8. The flowers on the table fit perfectly with the china and tablecloth.

   a. _____

   b. _____

   c. _____

9. That housing development was poorly built.

   a. _____

   b. _____

   c. _____

10. That baseball bat, signed by the team members, means a great deal to me.

    a. _____

    b. _____

    c. _____

Exercise 7-4:   Organizing details into paragraphs

DIRECTIONS: *Choose one of the three sets of details provided. Rearrange the details into a well-organized descriptive paragraph. Begin with an appropriate topic sentence.*

Invent additional details and revise these sentences as you think best. Remember to omit statements that you feel are irrelevant or inappropriate.

Group A

1. My car stereo is important in my car.

2. It helps me stay awake when I'm tired, and it keeps me from getting bored in traffic.

3. The stereo features Dolby Noise Reduction, auto-reverse tape deck, and twelve preset stations.

4. I know how important it is because right now it is broken, and I really miss it.

5. I received the stereo from my grandfather, and soon after that, he passed away.

6. Whenever I get into my car, I turn up the radio, and not a time goes by that I don't think of Grandpa.

7. The quality of the stereo equipment is not the best, but it does the job for me.

8. The brand name is Alpine, which is one of the best names in car stereos.

9. It is the size of a standard car radio, but it has more to offer than a regular one.

10. I am enjoying this stereo system a lot.

Group B

1. I have a female cat that I adore.

2. My family and I received her as a gift fifteen years ago when we lived in Mexico.

3. I became so intrigued by her and paid so much attention to her that over the years she has been referred to as "Bob's cat."

4. She is a white calico cat with black and brown patches.

5. We named her Patches because of her appearance.

6. She weighs about twenty pounds.

7. She is so fat that she looks misshapen.

8. Her cute little head looks tiny by comparison with her big body.

9. She looks like a plump polar bear with a tiny head.

10. She is eager for her food and begs by crying and looking up; with her eyes, she pleads for more.

11. She has a short, high-pitched "meow."

12. When I meow to her, she meows back as if to carry on a conversation.

Group C

1. A one-room cabin is across the river from my childhood home.

2. I am sure that the cabin was once a comfortable home.

3. The cabin stands desolate amid scrubby pines and unruly underbrush.

4. Aging wooden stairs lead up to the door.

5. The stairs creak and moan as I walk up to the door.

6. When I open the front door, I am overwhelmed by the musty, pungent aroma of decaying wood and upholstery.

7. Animals and vandals have ravaged the room.

8. An overstuffed sofa leans awkwardly against the wall.

9. Sofa cushions are scattered, and upholstery stuffing is coming through holes in the fabric.

10. A dust-covered afghan lies across the back of the sofa.

11. The afghan was made of bright-colored yarn.

12. It had been nicely crocheted.

13. The afghan probably was made by someone who had lived in the cabin.

14. Crocheting such a large piece must have taken many hours.

15. A red stone fireplace dominates the north wall.

16. People must have cooked meals in the cabin.

17. Bits of charred wood in the firebox suggest fires that once warmed the family and cooked the meals.

18. Old pots and pans hang from wooden pegs along the stone wall.

19. The pots and pans are now black because of use.

20. Dust, dirt, and spiders' webs now cover everything.

21. Old lace curtains, yellowed with age, cover the large bay window.

22. The late afternoon sun catches my attention.

23. I can almost hear the laughter of children playing on the river bank and the sounds of the evening meal being prepared in the cabin.

Exercise 7-5: Reading descriptive paragraphs for analysis and enjoyment

DIRECTIONS: *Read the descriptive paragraphs below carefully, enjoying the vivid pictures that come to mind. Notice that these paragraphs were written by professional authors; they are part of longer pieces of writing.*
Underline the details that appeal to your senses. Include not just sight, but all the senses. During class discussion, mention the specific details that stand out in your mind. Lines are numbered for easy reference.

Example 1

This paragraph comes from E. B. White's essay, "Once More to the Lake" (*Essays of E. B. White* [New York: Harper & Row, 1977], 200). Here the author describes a summer retreat that he had enjoyed in his youth:

1 Summertime, oh, summertime, pattern of life indelible, the fade-
2 proof lake, the woods unshatterable, the pasture with the sweetfern and
3 the juniper forever and ever, summer without end; this was the back-
4 ground, and the life along the shore was the design, the cottages with
5 their innocent and tranquil design, their tiny docks with the flagpole and
6 the American flag floating against the white clouds in the blue sky, the
7 little paths over the roots of the trees leading from camp to camp and at
8 the souvenir counters at the store the miniature birch-bark canoes and
9 the postcards that showed things looking a little better than they looked.
10 This was the American family at play, escaping the city heat, wondering
11 whether the newcomers in the camp at the head of the cove were "com-
12 mon" or "nice," wondering whether it was true that the people who drove
13 up for Sunday dinner at the farmhouse were turned away because there
14 wasn't enough chicken.

Example 2

This paragraph comes from *My Antonia,* a novel by Willa Cather (Boston: Houghton Mifflin, 1918), 137:

1   July came on with that breathless, brilliant heat which makes the
2   plains of Kansas and Nebraska the best corn country in the world. It
3   seemed as if we could hear the corn growing in the night; under the stars
4   one caught a faint crackling in the dewy, heavy-odoured [*sic*] cornfields
5   where the feathered stalks stood so juicy and green. If all the great plain
6   from the Missouri to the Rocky Mountains had been under glass, and the
7   heat regulated by a thermometer, it could not have been better for the
8   yellow tassels that were ripening and fertilizing the silk day by day. The
9   cornfields were far apart in those times, with miles of wild grazing land
10   between. It took a clear, meditative eye like my grandfather's to foresee
11   that they would enlarge and multiply until they would be, not the
12 . Shimerdas' cornfields, or Mr. Bushy's, but the world's cornfields; that
13   their yield would be one of the great economic facts, like the wheat crop
14   of Russia, which underlie all the activities of men, in peace or war.

Exercise 7-6:   Writing a descriptive paragraph

DIRECTIONS: *On separate paper, write a descriptive paragraph using any one of the topic ideas in Exercises 7-2 or 7-3, or on another topic of your choice.*

Here is another suggestion: Think of an object that has special meaning for you. It could be something you made, something given to you on a special occasion, something that has religious or family significance for you.

Describe that object with special emphasis on the meaning it has for you. The students' examples at the end of the chapter may give you ideas (the paragraphs on a special softball and on an A.A. medallion).

If your teacher so directs, bring your paragraph to class for peer evaluation. Use the questions in Chapter 10 or others suggested by your teacher as a basis for evaluation and discussion.

8

Writing Expository Paragraphs

Defining Expository Writing

Expository writing informs readers. The root word "expose" means "to display, reveal, or disclose; to lay open, make visible or known." Expository writing makes information known. It reveals information to readers.

You see expository writing every day in textbooks, cookbooks, how-to-do-it manuals, dictionaries, encyclopedias, and other reference books, magazines, and news reporting in the newspapers. Just think back over the past week. In those few days, you have learned many things you had not known. You might have used sources such as these for various kinds of information:

- a car owner's manual, to find out how to set the clock
- a cookbook, to get a recipe for baking a cake
- the yellow pages, to learn who repairs refrigerators nearby
- today's newspaper, to learn about a recent change in tax law
- the local radio station, to hear a weather forecast
- a television newscast, to find out who is running for mayor

Practice 8-1.   Recalling recently acquired information

DIRECTIONS: *What information have you learned during the past week?*
Give the source and the information, using the examples above as a pattern.

1. _____

   _____

2. _____

   _____

3. _____

   _____

   As a writer, you will sometimes inform readers by writing about your personal experiences. More often, however, you will go beyond first-hand experiences because those are limited. Knowledge of the external world, past and present, near and far—everything outside that "world" of your personal observation, memories, and feelings—is also knowledge you must prepare to write about.

   If you are writing a paper for a history class, you will probably study the material in your textbook and in assigned readings on reserve in the library. Then you will write a paper that demonstrates the knowledge and insight you have gained. Whether you study business, science and technology, the arts and humanities, sociology, education, or the other social sciences, your expository writing will be based upon study and observation, not direct first-hand experience. At times, however, your study may be enhanced by personal experience.

   Here are some examples of expository writing that would be based on first-hand experience:

- an employer's letter, to provide information about an employee's work record
- a student's lab report, to explain a biology experiment and describe the findings
- a memo from a tax auditor, to state findings of an audit

By contrast, these pieces of writing would be based on study and observation, perhaps enhanced by first-hand observation or experience:

- a historian's description of a Civil War battlefield, to explain how the terrain affected the outcome of the battle
- a stockbroker's letter to clients, to compare the performance of oil-company stocks last year with their performance this year
- a supervisor's memo, to explain her interpretation of company policies on sick leave

Sometimes it is impossible to know whether information is based on study or on experience, on first- or second-hand knowledge. In the list just before Practice 8-1, one who might have used first-hand experience is the cookbook writer, provided that person developed that recipe. Normally those who prepare reports for newspaper, radio, or television use information gathered by others; therefore, the reports are not based on direct experience of those who do the reporting.

Practice 8-2.   Examining sources of information

DIRECTIONS: *Look again at the list you made in Practice 8-1. Consider the writers who presented the information. To the best of your knowledge, which of those writers used first-hand personal experience as a basis for writing? List them on the lines below.*

_____

_____

Because expository writing is so much a part of your everyday life, you may not realize how common it really is. When you stop to think about it, you will recognize that expository prose includes a tremendous amount of writing, varied in length, form, and purpose.

You will find in this chapter some common patterns of organization used in exposition. In fact, writers can use any organizing pattern that helps readers understand the material. The patterns described in this chapter are useful at times, but no writer is limited to them.

The principle to remember is that **expository writing informs readers.** To accomplish that goal, you must make the information clear by using a logical pattern of organization.

Using Common Patterns

A pattern of organization is somewhat like a blueprint; it is a carefully considered plan for arranging materials. If a blueprint is designed well, the structure built from it will be attractive overall, and it will serve its intended purpose. Of course, no one has ready-made blueprints for all the buildings that might be erected. To get a good plan for a project, architects must take many factors into account, such as location, size, uses, and available resources.

Like a builder, you need a carefully considered plan for arranging materials when you write. You want a plan that results in an interesting piece of writing and one that conveys information in a clear, logical way. No one has ready-made patterns for all the expository writing that you might do. To get a good plan, you must take various factors into account, including your audience, purpose, information, and interpretation.

Although you must adapt to specific situations, you can start by considering standard patterns. The five patterns described in this chapter are common, and you will find them useful at times. They have proved serviceable to many writers for years—though only at some times, in some ways, on some topics. These patterns apply to longer pieces of writing as well. If you understand how they are used in paragraph writing, you can easily see that they could be expanded into multiparagraph pieces. You will find them helpful, but again—only at some times, in some ways, on some topics.

Comparison/Contrast

Writing with the comparison/contrast pattern, you examine similarities (comparisons) and differences (contrasts) between two people, objects, or ideas. The topic can be as abstract as socialism vs. capitalism, or it can be as concrete as Brand X vs. Brand Y toothpaste. Obviously for a single paragraph, the topic must be narrow enough to allow discussion of specific similarities and differences.

Although it is possible to consider only similarities or only differences, you will ordinarily think of both. It is hard not to think of both because usually, when comparing and contrasting, you are trying to make choices. You will always have purposes or reasons for making comparisons and contrasts. Often your purpose is to discover, then to show that one item or idea is better or more desirable than the other. To help readers understand why you think so, you may have to explain both similarities and differences.

For instance, you may wish to be in one of two places Friday night, but you can't seem to decide between the two. You might draw a line down the center of a paper and label the left side "Mike's party" and the right side "Work." You might think of all the reasons for going to Mike's party and write them down, then all the reasons for going to work and write them down, also. It's not that one choice is better than the other overall, but one may be better for specific reasons.

Once you have made your choice, you have a topic idea. If you decide to go to the party, the topic idea might be "Mike's party is a better choice because I will see friends from high school, people I rarely get to see." Or, if you decide to go to work, the topic idea might be, "I will go to work because I don't feel like trading my shift and I need the money."

Besides a topic idea, you would have specific supporting details on paper that might look something like this:

Mike's party	*Work*
Fun, relaxing	Supposed to work
Make new friends	Have to find substitute
See high-school friends for once	Might trade shifts
Seldom see them	Make good tips Friday nights
Have to get time off from work	Busy at work, time flies
Costs money not to work	Regulars come in
Good food	Nuisance to trade shifts
Good music	
Mike—good parties	

In effect, these lists illustrate brainstorming, a fine starting point. Your next step would be organizing that information. You could use one of these two methods for organizing the specific details:

- **block.** Each item is covered totally, first one and then the other. Main ideas are covered in the same order, first one item, then the other.

  For example, look at the left column below. Notice that all the information about Mike's party is presented in a block. Then all the information about work is presented in a second block.

- **point by point.** Each point of comparison is handled separately. The two items or concepts are considered in the same order throughout.

  For example, look at the right column below. Notice that the information about the party and about work is presented point by point: enjoying the evening, seeing people, and considering the cost.

Block	**Point by point**
Mike's party	*Enjoying Friday evening*
Enjoyment	Mike's party—fun, good food
Good food, music	Work—at least time goes fast
Relaxing, fun	
Seeing people	*Seeing people*
Make new friends	Mike's party—new friends and old
See old friends	Work—see Friday regulars
Considering cost	
Take time off from work	
Good tips on Fridays	

Work	*Considering cost*
Enjoyment	Mike's party—no earnings Friday
Time goes fast on Fridays	Work—good tips
Seeing people	
See regular customers	
Considering cost	
Good tips, lots of customers	

After you have arranged your ideas in either block or point-by-point sketches, such as those shown above, writing a well-organized paragraph is a matter of following the order of the items listed. Organizing is easier when you jot down just a few words, not entire sentences. The sketches are not formal outlines, though they could be expanded into that form. For informal writing, brief sketches will serve your purpose.

Practice 8-3.   Organizing details in block and point-by-point patterns

DIRECTIONS: *On separate paper, complete the block and point-by-point listings below. Use these details and any others you care to add:*

Brand A toothpaste:	mint flavoring
	tartar control
	recommended by dentists
	$1.39 for 6 oz. in tube (.23/oz.)
	$1.89 for 6 oz. in pump (.32/oz.)
	available at local supermarket
Brand B toothpaste:	no flavoring
	designed for sensitive teeth
	recommended by dentists
	$2.49 for 6 oz. (.42/oz.)
	not available in pump
	available at drugstores

Block	**Point by point**
Brand A	*Reasons for use*
Reasons for use	Brand A
Convenience	Brand B
Cost	
	Convenience
Brand B	Brand A
Reasons for use	Brand B
Convenience	
Cost	*Cost*
	Brand A
	Brand B

Practice 8-4.   Developing ideas for comparison/contrast writing

DIRECTIONS: *On separate paper, list similarities and differences on a topic of interest to you. You might consider such topics as these:*

- *one specific product vs. another: cars, articles of clothing, sports equipment, housewares, or others*
- *choices a student makes: college, majors, elective courses, or others*
- *choices related to recreation: movies, musicians or music groups, types of dances, travel options, or others*
- *work-related topics: fixed vs. flexible benefits, full-time vs. part-time jobs, no-smoking vs. freedom-to-smoke environment, or others*
- *your expectations vs. reality: expectations of the prom, military service, a specific job, a wedding or other family occasion vs. how things really turned out.*

Arrange the ideas according to one of the two methods, block or point by point. Bring your papers to class for peer-group discussion. Look for other ideas that might be included, and consider whether each point you have is worth including.

Write a paragraph based on your revised plan.

Process

To explain how a task is done, we use a technique called process writing. Most authors of "how-to" books use process writing. The order is normally chronological, step by step, so that the reader can follow the directions in the order in which they are given. Many times descriptive writing is used to help readers form mental pictures of tools or supplies or how to shape materials.

Process writing does not necessarily deal with concrete tasks that involve tangible tools. Some process writing does exactly that, of course, teaching readers how to handle tasks ranging from cooking to plumbing to car repair, among other things. But other process writing deals with improving your health or life-style (such as self-improvement books), how to achieve a goal (such as get-rich-quick books), or how to improve what you are already doing (such as money-management guides).

To tell anyone how to do anything, you must first know the procedure well yourself. Knowing, however, is one thing; explaining so that others can understand is something else. Therein lies the challenge in process writing. Generally, you will explain well if you keep readers' needs in mind. Awareness of your readers will encourage you to follow these guidelines:

- Give complete information—all the tools, supplies, equipment, and materials, and all the steps.
- Take readers through the steps in order.
- Go into greater detail over difficult or unfamiliar terms or procedures.
- Recall your experiences as a beginner and alert readers to common mistakes.
- Warn readers of hazards.

No one can tell you exactly how much explaining is needed about tools or steps. Consider the readers, the process itself, and your purpose in explaining. Sometimes you want readers to be able to duplicate the steps you are explaining. At other times, you simply want them to understand how the procedure is done. Naturally, if you are helping readers to go through the steps themselves, you have to be more explicit in giving directions.

Because of the topic she chose, the student who wrote the paragraph below had very little to explain about equipment. For serious runners, good shoes are one essential requirement; therefore, the writer discusses shoes before she gets into the system of training for long-distance races:

[1]Training for a marathon requires careful preparation and steady, gradual increases in the length of the runs. [2]Before you begin, buy the best-fitting, best-built running shoes you can find. [3]No one can say which brand will work best for you or feel best on your feet, so you have to rely on your experience and on the feel of each pair as you shop. [4]When you have found shoes that seem right, walk in them for a few days to double-check the fit. [5]If they still feel good, you can begin running in them. [6]As always, you should stretch at least ten minutes before each run to prevent injuries and soreness. [7]During the first week, do not think about distance, but run five minutes longer each day. [8]After six days, it is wise to take a day off to rest, but during that next week, set a goal of at least a mile and a half per run. [9]With each day, increase the distance by a half mile. [10]After two weeks, start timing yourself. [11]You are ready to figure out a goal for improving distance and time. [12]Depending on the kind of race you plan to enter, you can set up a timetable for the remaining weeks before the race.

Practice 8-5. Analyzing a process paragraph

DIRECTIONS: *Answer these questions about the paragraph above.*

1. Which is the topic sentence? _____

2. Which sentences pertain to supplies or materials to be assembled before

   the procedure begins? _____

3. In which sentences does the writer provide warnings about possible

   hazards? _____

4. At many points in the paragraph, readers are aware of the passing of
   time. Using sentence numbers for quick answers, list three places in
   which the chronology is apparent:

   _____

5. Underline transitional words and phrases in the paragraph.

Sometimes you can make your point more effectively by taking a humorous or whimsical approach. You can use a device called "irony." With this technique, your words will convey a point exactly the opposite of their literal meaning.

Suppose you want a friend (someone still in high school, perhaps) to understand the need for self-discipline when going to college. If you give the usual straightforward advice, your statements will be predictable: attend classes regularly, pay attention in class, keep up with your homework, and so on. By using irony, a student writer made all these points, but in a much more memorable way:

Failing in college is easy if you follow these simple directions. First, sign up for early morning courses even though you work until midnight four nights a week. When the term begins, be sure to miss the first three or four days. In this way you can start out behind everyone else. Don't worry about catching up; you have too many other things to think about. Then, after the first week, skip class at least once a week, or better yet, twice a week. When you are in class, pretend to pay attention, but daydream instead. If the classroom has windows, look outside even if there is nothing to look at. Most important, never study. You can always go out with friends, see a movie, or go to a ballgame. If not, watch television or call friends on the phone. Whatever you do, ignore your homework, and don't bother reading the textbooks. If you follow my advice, you will surely fail, probably within one term or less.

Practice 8-6.   Generating ideas for a process paragraph

DIRECTIONS: *Select a process you know well. Brainstorm about the steps in that process. Consider how you would guide a beginner through them. List items you should include.*

You might consider topics such as these:

- Giving directions for a process on the job
    - Opening or closing the cash register for the day
    - Writing up an invoice or shipping order
    - Operating the dishwasher
    - Getting help in an emergency (specify the type of emergency)
    - Admitting a patient

- Giving directions for a process not related to work
    - Selecting a color-coordinated outfit
    - Planting or pruning a tree or shrub
    - Getting a driver's license or marriage license
    - Installing tiles, caulking windows, or replacing shingles (or other maintenance tasks)
    - Planning a menu for a diabetic or a person on some other special diet

- Taking a humorous, whimsical, or ironic approach
    - How to lose a friend (or ruin some other relationship)
    - How to slip into chemical dependency
    - How to get into debt

Bring your list to class for peer evaluation. After revising your ideas, write a process paragraph.

Classification

To categorize types of people or things, you can use classification writing. You show, with classification, that the types are distinct from one another, and you explain enough characteristics of each type to allow the reader to understand the differences.

When you classify, you work with subdivisions or types of people or things, such as types of recruiting officers, managers of fast-food restaurants, football fans, flowering house plants, chocolate bars, or ski boots. Begin with a group of people or things, then narrow that topic. You could begin with the very big group "cars," but then narrow "cars" to "sports cars," or better still, "American-made sports cars produced in the last two years."

After you narrow the topic, create categories into which you can place individual items. Remember that one common denominator should be used for sorting the items into categories: You could sort American-built sports cars according to price, performance, or manufacturer. Individual cars would then be placed in the appropriate category.

It is very important to use *one* common denominator for sorting so that all the items will fit into one and only one category. If you use price as the common denominator for sorting sports cars into categories, each car will fit into one price range; it will be in that one category and no other. Most often, three or four separate categories are set up. If the topic has been sufficiently narrowed, these should be enough.

Practice 8-7.   Analyzing categories for use in classification

DIRECTIONS: *Consider this example and answer the questions that follow. A student decided to classify drivers, using these four categories:*

truck drivers
bus drivers
poor drivers
women drivers

1. Did the student use a common denominator for dividing drivers into

   these categories? _____

   If so, what was it? _____

2. The phrase "poor drivers" is vague. If the writer had started with dangerous drivers as a common denominator, what categories might he have used?

   _____

   _____

3. Ideally, the categories are set up so that each item will fit into only one category. Look at the student's categories again. How many of those might the same person fit into?

As Practice 8-7 demonstrates, you can see the flaws in someone else's plans quite easily. The real challenge is in setting up categories to use in your own classification paragraph. Remember these two steps:

1. Narrow the topic
2. Use one common denominator

If you begin with the general topic of restaurant food, first narrow your focus to one kind of restaurant. You could use any one of these: ethnic restaurants, fast-food restaurants, buffets, diners, or other kinds. After some thought, you might decide to focus on ethnic restaurants, then specifically those featuring Chinese food.

Next, think about the menu selections and separate them into types, according to some common denominator. You might use the method of cooking (stir-fried, steamed, baked, and so on), or you might use the main ingredient in the selections (meat-based, vegetable-based, rice- or noodle-based dishes). You could use some other common denominator, so long as you sort all the items by the same criterion.

In writing a classification paragraph, you will focus on the common denominator, but you will add other information as well. One student's common denominator is the way in which customers tip in the restaurant where she works. The several types are apparent from her description. Notice the information included about each type of customer and the transitions that guide readers from one type to another:

[1]As a waitress at a popular bar and grill, I see a lot of differences in the tips my customers give me. [2]The worst kind of customer is the "stiffer." [3]These are the most demanding and impatient people to serve, and then they leave me nothing. [4]A step above the stiffers are the "el cheapo" customers, who must think they are great tippers. [5]If an "el cheapo" orders a $5.95 pitcher of beer, I'll get $6 and be told to keep the change. [6]Even so, these customers let me know they expect quick service. [7]The next type is the standard tipper, who leaves the normal 15 percent tip. [8]The standard tipper tends to be quiet and orderly, a "normal"-appearing customer in every way. [9]These people are always welcome,

especially after I deal with the other two types. [10]But in the last category we find generous tippers, every waiter's dream come true. [11]These customers are the ones who order a $5.95 pitcher of beer and pay $8 with a cheerful "keep the change," even if the beer happened to come through slowly. [12]To make things even nicer, these customers order the rest of the evening, adding big tips every time. [13]The variety makes my job interesting, but I have to admit I like the last two types best.

Practice 8-8.   Analyzing a classification paragraph

DIRECTIONS: *Answer these questions about the paragraph above.*

1. Which is the topic sentence? _____

2. Besides the amount of the tip, what kinds of information did the writer

   give about members of each category? _____

   _____

3. Look at the four types of customers again. The student could have pre-

   sented the types in some other order. Which order did she use? _____

   _____

4. What other order might have been used? _____

   _____

5. In your opinion, would the paragraph have been more or less interesting if the writer had started with the most generous tippers and ended
   with the least generous? Why?

   _____

   _____

Classification differs from comparison/contrast in two ways:
First, the material is different. In classification, you discuss types of a plural entity, such as types of sports cars, types of customers, types of restaurant food. You will probably deal with three or four types or categories.

In comparison/contrast, you discuss two—only two—distinct entities or ideas, such as brand X vs. brand Y; American-made sports cars vs. European-made sports cars; attending Friday night's party vs. working that night.

Second, the purpose is different. When you classify, you want readers to recognize types of items or people. To help them do so, you point out distinctive characteristics of each type. Readers will draw their own conclusions, perhaps making mental comparisons between items in the categories. In comparison/contrast, you deliberately point out similarities and differences. Often you want readers to see the advantages or desirability of one over the other, and you guide your readers' thinking by the way in which you present the material.

Practice 8-9.   Planning a classification paragraph

DIRECTIONS: *Select a general topic, such as those listed below. Then narrow it for use in a classification paragraph.*

General topics

- People—supervisors, coworkers, neighbors, teachers, clergy, doctors, customers, boyfriends or girlfriends, sports fans
- Things—articles of clothing, shoes, cosmetics, restaurant food, cars, boats, sports equipment, house plants, television shows, movies, musical groups

On separate paper, set up categories into which the items will fit without overlapping. Bring your paper to class for discussion and peer evaluation.

After revising your plans, write a paragraph.

Cause and Effect

A logical method much used by writers is the cause/effect sequence, which deals with either cause or effect or both, often in chronological order. Causes eventually lead to effects, and so if you are writing about the accumulating influence of some cause, you will be moving forward in time. The opposite is true with effects: because effects can be traced back to causes, you will be reaching back in time, explaining what happened earlier.

Consider the causes and effects in this student's account of an accident:

¹I had just returned from lunch when my boss told me to help set up for the warehouse sale. ²First I was supposed to take all the old wallpaper out of the top bins. ³I found the forklift and got a skid (a platform for holding the wallpaper). ⁴Soon I had the skid at the top of the bin, ready to be loaded. ⁵I set the parking brake on the forklift so that I would feel safe standing so many feet in the air. ⁶Then I climbed to the top of the bin and began loading the skid. ⁷When it was about half full, I heard a cracking sound, and the next thing I knew, I was falling. ⁸There was nothing to grab to stop the fall. ⁹I hit the cement floor, landing directly on my knees. ¹⁰A crowd of coworkers gathered around and asked if I was okay. ¹¹I was hurting, but not so much right then. ¹²I tried to stand up, but I couldn't, so I was rushed to the hospital. ¹³After x-rays and tests, the doctor concluded that I had damaged the cartilage in my knees. ¹⁴She said I would never water-ski or downhill-ski again, but that I would walk normally in time. ¹⁵I have paid a big price just because a skid broke under the weight of seventy pounds of wallpaper.

Practice 8-10.   Analyzing a cause/effect paragraph

DIRECTIONS: *Answer these questions about the paragraph above.*

1. Which sentence serves as a topic sentence? _____

2. Which sentences lead up to the accident, establishing causes for the

   writer's fall? _____

3. Which sentences deal with the effects of the fall?

   _____

4. Why does the writer include a brief definition in sentence 3?

   _____

5. Underline transitional words and phrases in the paragraph.

6. Notice that a narrative is used here to explain cause or effect. Besides the chronological order, what elements of narrative writing do you see here?

_____

_____

_____

As the example preceding Practice 8-10 shows, a writer can deal with both cause and effect. That sample paragraph is divided almost evenly between cause and effect. At other times, a piece of writing might be focused primarily on one or the other. For instance, in this student's paragraph, the writer focuses on the causes for the action she finally took. Her ending states the effect or result of the "causes":

Almost every morning, long before I was ready to wake up, I was shaken out of my sleep by the roar of a Boeing 747 going over my building. Sometimes the sound waves rattled my window. When I opened my eyes, I always looked at the clock. It might read 6:10 or even earlier! The earlier it was, the more disgusted I was. But that wasn't the worst part of the airplane noise. Maybe I could have gotten used to waking up early, but I could never get used to constant interruptions all day. It seemed like every time I got on the phone, another plane would fly over. I couldn't hear a thing the caller was saying, and the caller couldn't hear me. Every time I settled down to enjoy a favorite television program, the same thing would happen. The roar of the engines ruined some of the best moments in my favorite programs. Finally, I had suffered enough. I like my apartment and my neighbors, but I was forced to move to a quieter part of town.

In cause/effect writing, you will often find that chronological order works well, but that arrangement is not required. You might find that your ideas work better if you move from the least significant to the most significant cause or effect. In the next student's paragraph, the emphasis is on effects growing out of a cause (smoking). Notice that the writer gives a sense of chronology but also moves from the least to the most important effects:

¹I wish I had never started smoking. ²I began at age sixteen, and I got suspended from school for smoking. ³Before long, I had less interest in school. ⁴For one thing, I was in trouble over smoking. ⁵Also, I needed to work more. ⁶It seems like I was always buying cigarettes, not just for me but for my smoking buddies, too. ⁷Another serious result was the misery I caused my parents. ⁸They begged me to stop smoking. ⁹But I wouldn't stop, and the habit took hold more and more. ¹⁰Now I wish I could stop. ¹¹Every day I wake up with a terrible taste in my mouth, and a lot of days I also have a sore throat. ¹²Next the coughing starts. ¹³By the middle of the morning, I promise myself that I will quit. ¹⁴I know the dangers of smoking, but I also know the power of its control over me.

Practice 8-11.   Analyzing a cause/effect paragraph

DIRECTIONS: *Answer these questions about the paragraph above:*

1. As a reader, how do you know that you are moving forward in time?

   _____

   _____

2. The writer mentions several effects smoking has had on his life. Which of these effects is most serious is a matter of opinion, but in general, do you sense that he arranged the effects from least to most serious? Or are the effects organized in this way for some other reason?

   _____

   _____

3. Though he does not say so directly, the writer is more disturbed about effects on his health than about effects on his financial condition. How does the writer indicate the relative importance of various effects?

   _____

   _____

4. Coherence is ensured partly by transitional words and phrases and partly by pronoun reference and repetition of key words. Underline examples of pronoun reference and repetition of key words in the paragraph.

The students' paragraphs above show that first-hand experience can be used in paragraphs based on cause and effect. But many topics used in cause/effect writing reflect study and observation beyond any one writer's personal experience. Consider the knowledge required for discussing topics like these:

- causes of an illness, deformity, or injury
- causes of a specific environmental problem; social, economic, political, or other national problems
- effects of an illness, deformity, or injury
- effects of instances of poor judgment, including choice of friends, jobs, life-style
- effects of an environmental hazard; homelessness, child abuse, divorce, indebtedness; or some other social or personal problem.

Practice 8-12.   Generating ideas for a cause/effect paragraph

DIRECTIONS: *Select a topic for a cause/effect paragraph. You may use items in the list above, provided you have enough knowledge to write about the topic. Then narrow the topic so that you can get into detail.*

On separate paper, brainstorm for ideas suitable for your cause/effect paragraph. Bring your list of ideas to class for discussion. After revising, write a paragraph.

Definition

Normally, definitions are very brief—just enough to explain a term or concept that is either unfamiliar or being used in an unusual sense. A sentence or two can provide a workable definition. In fact, a few words inserted in parentheses might be enough, as you saw when the writer explained in the cause/effect paragraph above that a "skid" was a platform for holding wallpaper.

Sometimes, however, an entire paragraph (or even several paragraphs) will be devoted to an "extended definition" of a term. Because of the greater length, readers naturally expect that one meaning (or perhaps several meanings) will be elaborated upon.

The purpose of extended definition is to explain a word or concept in detail, often revealing special, perhaps personal interpretations. You have a lot of freedom in explaining meanings. Generally, you will use a combination of devices, including any pattern of organization discussed previously.

In Paragraphs A and B below, both writers attempt to define the word "friend." In Paragraph A, notice that the writer is vague and general. Because she neglects to give examples or details, readers do not know exactly what she means:

Paragraph A

¹A friend is a person with whom I can dare to be myself. ²I can say what I really think, and I know my friend won't criticize me. ³I can complain to a friend when I am upset. ⁴I can cry if I feel like it, and I don't have to explain why. ⁵A good friend just lets me be free. ⁶I can be myself and express whatever I feel. ⁷I don't have to worry about being different. ⁸I also don't have to worry about being ignored when I am having rough times. ⁹I can go to a friend and talk through my problems. ¹⁰A good friend is willing to listen and try to understand. ¹¹A good friend lets me be myself.

By contrast, in Paragraph B, the writer gives more specific information. She also uses classification to organize her ideas.

Paragraph B

¹The meaning of "friend" depends on the closeness of the relationship. ²I have lots of friends, a couple of close girlfriends, and one special boyfriend. ³In the first category, I'd include a number of people I've met at work, in my apartment complex, and at school. ⁴We talk and share jokes, and sometimes we go to the movies or go shopping together. ⁵We enjoy being together, but we don't share serious thoughts too much. ⁶In the next category, I'd include two friends, Katie and Jackie, whom I have known for many years. ⁷They are the ones I call if I'm upset and need to talk over problems, fears, and inner secrets. ⁸I'll never forget when I called Katie and told her how I got fired. ⁹She just listened, and we talked until I started to feel a little better. ¹⁰The last category has only one very special friend, my boyfriend Brad. ¹¹We are so close that we can almost read each other's mind. ¹²We are quick to support each other with encouragement and gratitude, remaining open to the other's feelings. ¹³Anyone who has the experience of friendship on several levels can understand how much all my friends mean to me. ¹⁴Though they are all different, each has an important place in my life.

Practice 8-13.   Examining definition paragraphs

DIRECTIONS: *The* American Heritage Dictionary *defines the word "friend" in these ways:*

> *A person whom one knows, likes, and trusts. Any associate or acquaintance. A favored companion: a boy friend or girl friend.*

Though the writers of Paragraphs A and B above do not quote the dictionary, they express some of the dictionary meanings. In which sentences do the writers convey these meanings?

1. A person whom one knows, likes, and trusts.

   Sentences _____ in Paragraph A

   Sentences _____ in Paragraph B

2. Any associate or acquaintance.

   Sentences _____ in Paragraph A

   Sentences _____ in Paragraph B

3. A favored companion.

   Sentences _____ in Paragraph A

   Sentences _____ in Paragraph B

4. In Paragraph B, what is the common denominator used to set individuals into the three categories? _____

5. Which sentences express the topic ideas?

   Paragraph A _____ Paragraph B _____

6. One paragraph gives a much better understanding of the word "friend" than the other. Which paragraph is better, and in what ways? _____

   _____

Although it is not necessary to use the dictionary to define, sometimes you will want to quote a particularly helpful portion of a dictionary definition. If that portion fits into your ideas and helps you make a point, you have good reason to use it. Remember to use quotation marks to set off borrowed words. Also remember to be selective about what you quote, knowing that readers are easily bored by quoted definitions; besides, if you are not careful, part of the dictionary definition can lead away from the main point in your paper.

In this paragraph, the writer does a good job of gracefully weaving a quotation into his paragraph:

> [1]You have only fifty cents on a hot, dry day, yet a can of cold soda pop costs fifty-five cents. [2]The feeling you experience is a mild case of an emotion called "frustration." [3]The dictionary would have us believe that frustration means "a deep chronic sense or state of insecurity and dissatisfaction arising from unresolved problems." [4]Dissatisfaction?! [5]That is not even half of what I feel when frustrated. [6]I feel rage welling up in me because I am helpless. [7]Instead of talking in sentences, I grunt, sputter a few words, and make empty hand gestures. [8]My mind is racing, but I'm unable to come up with a solution. [9]My pulse may quicken, and my breathing may become quick and shallow. [10]Frustration goes far beyond a "state of insecurity and dissatisfaction" into dismay and anger. [11]Finally, I throw up my hands, let out a giant sigh, and say "Oh, I give up!"

Practice 8-14.   Analyzing a definition paragraph

DIRECTIONS: *Answer these questions about the paragraph above:*

1. What purpose is served by the opening sentence? _____

_____

2. Which sentence comes closest to being a standard topic sentence? _____

3. What purposes are served by the dictionary definition? _____

_____

_____

4. Lively, vivid details are used to show how the writer reacts when feeling frustration. List a few of those details. _____

_____

5. Create a new sentence using the material in sentences 4 and 5. (In doing so, you will get rid of the sentence fragment in 4.)

_____

_____

6. Your new sentence (the answer to question 5) gets rid of a sentence fragment. Now, in your opinion, which is more effective, your new sentence or the original version, including the fragment? _____

Why? _____

_____

As the paragraph above shows, lively exact details carry much weight in extended definitions. The paragraph would have been even better if the writer had given us examples of frustrations that made him feel helpless and angry. Examples are always helpful, but even more so when an abstract word, such as "friend," is discussed.

In these few sentences, a student offers examples to support her understanding of the abstract expression "self-esteem":

Self-esteem boils down to whether we are happy with ourselves. What it takes for a person to be happy with himself or herself depends a lot on the peer group. For teen-agers, having the right clothes, the right hairstyle, and being in the right group seems to create that sense of self-esteem. Later on, self-esteem apparently comes from having the right kind of job and living in the right part of town.

Whether or not you agree with the student's view of self-esteem, you are able to understand the connections she makes between self-esteem and the peer group.

As a last look at definition, consider the pattern of formal definitions, such as those found in dictionaries. A distinct pattern is followed, consisting of these three parts:

Term	Category	Distinguishing features
fuchsia	a tropical plant	having showy, drooping, purplish, reddish, or white flowers
divining rod	a forked branch or stick	allegedly indicating underground water by bending downward when held over the source

Notice that the category is fairly precise. A fuchsia isn't just a "thing that grows," or even just a "plant," but a specific kind of plant. You may have heard faulty definitions that use "is when" or "is where" instead of a category. Consider these faulty definitions:

Illogical: A divining rod is when you hold a stick over the ground and let it point to water.

Illogical: A divining rod is where you hold a stick over the ground and let it point to water.

When you stop to think about it, you realize that a divining rod cannot be defined with "is when" or "is where" because a divining rod is not a time or a place, but rather a forked stick.

In almost all definitions, the "distinguishing features" section requires more explanation than the rest of the definition put together. The "distinguishing features" separate the item from all others in the same category. Thus, the fuchsia is separated from other tropical shrubs by the specific characteristics mentioned in the "distinguishing features" part of the definition.

You can create your own definitions, following that pattern. Whether or not you use your own formal definition in a paragraph, you can use this pattern while brainstorming for an extended definition paper. You might start like this:

Term	Category	Distinguishing features
love	emotion	overwhelming, forever, wonderful
justice	idea	based on fairness, disagreed upon often, basis for many fights

Of course, these definitions are not complete, but they represent a typical start toward an extended definition.

Practice 8-15.   Creating formal definitions

DIRECTIONS: *See how well you can define these common words, using the pattern above. Do not consult the dictionary; rather, see what you can do on your own. Write on separate paper.*

Term	Category	Distinguishing features
1. chair		
2. backpack		
3. prejudice		

When writing an extended definition, you can draw upon formal definitions from the dictionary or definitions you have created. You can use comparison and contrast, showing how the term is similar to or different from closely related words. You might use process writing to show the development of a concept (such as self-esteem). You could use classification to show types, as one student did with the word "friend." You might need cause/effect writing to explain an expression (such as acid rain).

You have the same options, whether you are writing an extended definition or any other expository prose. You can combine methods, drawing upon those which will help the reader understand your ideas. Brief definitions fit in many pieces of writing, as do points of comparison and contrast. Whenever you convey information to readers in a clear, logical way, making sure the reader can understand easily and fully, you are creating good expository writing.

Summary

- Expository writing informs and explains. "Expository" comes from the root verb "expose," meaning to reveal, to make known, to disclose.

- Expository writing can follow many patterns of organization. The important thing is that the ideas are arranged in clear, logical order.

- Comparison/contrast writing shows similarities and differences between two people, ideas, or things. Comparing means showing similarities; contrasting means showing differences.

- Comparison/contrast can be organized by using either the block or the point-by-point method. In the block method, one item is discussed thoroughly, then the other. In the point-by-point method, each point of comparison or contrast is discussed, item by item.

- Process writing explains how something is done. It often gives readers the directions they need to complete the procedure themselves.

- Classification writing presents categories or types of people or things. Items are placed in categories according to a common denominator. Then each category is discussed with sufficient detail to make its characteristics clear.

- Cause/effect writing explores causes or effects or both. A chronological arrangement of ideas is frequently appropriate. Moving from the least to most important (or the reverse) might also be appropriate in cause/effect writing.

- Extended definition means a paragraph or more of discussion about a term or concept.

- A formal definition consists of the term itself, a category into which the term fits, and the distinguishing features of that term.

- Writers can combine patterns of organization in whatever ways seem best.

Exercise 8-1:   Selecting organizing patterns for topics

DIRECTIONS: *Suppose that you were planning to write about each of the topics listed below. Which of these patterns of organization would you use?*

comparison/contrast
process
classification
cause/effect
definition

Write your choice on the line after each topic, and explain that choice briefly. For some topics, more than one pattern might work.

Example

Topic: The making of a hurricane
Pattern: Process, explaining that wind, moisture, and air pressure go through distinct stages as a hurricane develops

1. Changes in wheat farming from 1900 to the present

_____

_____

2. How osteoporosis affected my grandmother's life

_____

_____

3. Why osteoporosis affects only some individuals

_____

_____

4. The significance of oncogenes in cancer research

_____

_____

5. Research procedures that led to the discovery of oncogenes

_____

_____

6. Types of rocks found on the moon

_____

_____

7. Warning signs that a person is contemplating suicide

_____

_____

8. The meaning of "impressionism" as applied to French painting in the late nineteenth century

_____

_____

9. Impressionism vs. expressionism in painting

_____

_____

10. The prognosis for leukemia patients in 1965 vs. 1990

_____

_____

Exercise 8-2:   Analyzing students' paragraphs

DIRECTIONS: *On separate paper, answer these questions about each of the paragraphs below:*

1. Which pattern of organization is found in the paragraph?
2. Which is the topic sentence?
3. Does the writer use chronology? descriptive details? examples? an arrangement of ideas from most important (or best) to least important (or worst) or the reverse?
4. How has the writer ensured coherence? Cite specific uses of these devices:
   a. transitional words and phrases
   b. pronoun reference
   c. parallelism
   d. repetition of key words or ideas
5. As a reader, do you find the paragraph interesting or appealing? Why or why not?

Paragraph 1

[1]I guess the most important step in staying engaged is overlooking a fiancé's many flaws. [2]When he asks that cherished question, "Will you marry me?" just say yes. [3]Ignore the fact that he is so drunk he doesn't know which finger to put the engagement ring on. [4]Forget that you co-signed the loan on the ring. [5]Once you do, the real fun rolls along because now that you're engaged, he wants to move in with you. [6]He says that living together will cement the relationship. [7]It's just coincidence that he was evicted from his apartment and can't afford another place. [8]Cohabitation will be romantic: he'll cook, clean, and spend your money. [9]You find out pretty fast that he can't cook and he's too important to clean, but he is only too glad to spend your money. [10]If you want to stay engaged, you overlook all these flaws, but you have a harder time when

he wants to buy a car on your credit. [11]If you overlook that, you'll soon have even more to overlook. [12]But even if he drinks too much, spends your money, and ignores you and your opinions most of the time, isn't it better to be engaged than to be single? [13]After all, love has a way of working things out, or if not, love and credit cards will.

Paragraph 2

[1]It looks like a lot of confusion surrounds the slang word "dizwad." [2]Actually, the term has great meaning, especially if we look at it as a fusion of fragmented words that we all know. [3]The word "dizwad" can be split in half and considered in parts. [4]The fragment "diz" comes from the word "dizzy," meaning either that a person feels faint as if his or her head is spinning, or the physical sensation of fainting. [5]The slang meaning of "diz" refers to lack of mental capacity; in other words, "diz" means stupid or light in the head. [6]The person to whom that meaning would apply would not be the brightest around. [7]The other part, "wad" comes from the normal meaning of a wad as a mass, lump, or ball of something, like a wad of chewing gum. [8]Now we must make a mental leap and assume this ball of something is the person's brain. [9]Together, the fragment "diz" and the word "wad" make a vivid but negative picture of someone.

Paragraph 3

[1]If your vision requires help, you should think carefully about all the advantages of contact lenses before you buy eyeglasses. [2]First, glasses can be more expensive. [3]Frames and lenses are priced separately, and the frames alone can cost a lot if you order something that has style and looks nice. [4]Second, glasses are easily scratched or broken. [5]They are bulky, and you will have to watch out for them or they will slide, get bumped off your face, or get scratched by close contact with some object. [6]Most of all, glasses are a nuisance. [7]You may have to return to the store several times to get them adjusted right. [8]Later on, they will get wet, foggy, and dirty, because they pick up whatever is in your environment. [9]Contact lenses, by contrast, are often not as expensive, though the cost does depend upon the prescription. [10]The contact lenses are not so readily scratched or broken because they rest securely on the eye itself. [11]If you are carrying them

around, they are small and easy to handle, not bulky like glasses. [12]Best of all, contacts are easy to wear. [13]After a short adjustment period, they are almost unnoticed by the wearer. [14]If you try contact lenses, you will enjoy their many advantages over glasses.

Paragraph 4

[1]About a year ago I had an accident that has changed my life a lot. [2]My buddy Steve was coming to my house to pick me up to go to a hockey game. [3]I had warned him about the ice on our front steps so that he wouldn't slip and fall. [4]When Steve arrived, he came inside to use the phone, and then we were on our way. [5]As we were going out to his car, I took the worst fall of my life on the steps I had warned him about, falling four feet straight down onto my spine over the hard cement. [6]I had never felt so much pain as I felt in my back that night. [7]The accident couldn't have happened at a worse time. [8]I was on the varsity basketball team, and we were on our way to the best record in years. [9]For the first two weeks after my fall, I couldn't play at all, and I feared that my playing was over forever. [10]I saw several doctors, and they all said the same thing, "You're lucky. [11]Your back is going to be just fine." [12]But I was so sore that I could hardly move. [13]I did get back to playing after a few weeks, but I never let myself forget about being so stupid around those steps.

Paragraph 5

[1]During the ten months I've worked at an apartment rental office, I've found a way to size up prospective tenants. [2]It all depends on when they come looking vs. when they need the apartment. [3]The most desirable renters plan ahead. [4]They look at least a month in advance, and I assume that they are giving their present landlords the proper rental notice. [5]Although they may be a little picky about the condition of the apartment, it is easier for me to show them something they would like, simply because I have more time to work with them. [6]The next type of renter is seeking to rent within a month of my speaking to them. [7]This kind is easygoing and not worried about the condition of the apartment. [8]In fact, these people will help the maintenance crew by cleaning up after the former tenants, and they do not worry about little things. [9]The last kind

of renter wants to move in at once. [10]I can rent the least desirable apartments to these people because they are not fussy at all. [11]The reason they are not fussy is that they are so messy and irresponsible themselves. [12]Other tenants complain about them because they're usually so loud. [13]I dread these people too, because I know that they will leave without giving proper notice, and they will probably leave messes behind.

Exercise 8-3:   Writing a comparison/contrast paragraph

DIRECTIONS: *Write a comparison/contrast paragraph on a topic of your choice or one of the topics suggested in Practice 8-4, page 159.*
    At the top of your paper, write "block" or "point by point" to indicate your method of organization. If your teacher so directs, use your paragraph for peer evaluation in class. Be prepared to explain why you chose the point-by-point or block method.

Exercise 8-4:   Writing a process paragraph

DIRECTIONS: *Write a process paragraph on a topic of your choice or one of the topics suggested in Practice 8-6, page 162.*

Exercise 8-5:   Writing a classification paragraph

DIRECTIONS: *Write a classification paragraph on a topic of your choice or one of the topics suggested in Practice 8-9, page 166. Use three or four categories and distinguish them from one another by citing specific characteristics.*
    At the top of the paper, indicate the common denominator you used to separate people or things into categories.

Exercise 8-6:   Writing a cause/effect paragraph

DIRECTIONS: *Write a cause/effect paragraph on a topic of your choice or one of the topics you worked on in Practice 8-12, page 170.*
    At the top of the paper, indicate whether you are explaining both cause and effect or emphasizing one or the other.

Exercise 8-7:   Writing a definition paragraph

DIRECTIONS: *Write a definition paragraph on a topic of your choice or one of the topics suggested below.*

You may use part of a dictionary definition (inside quotation marks), but do not rely much on the dictionary. Invent your own definition, backing it up with examples. You may point out what the term does not mean, contrasting this term with a similar term or concept. You may classify or mention cause/effect relationships, if that helps you to explain. In short, use any combination of methods that you feel works well.

Suggested Topics

An abstract term, such as friendship, kindness, love, prejudice, self-esteem, despair, generosity, tact, patriotism, hate, and so on.

A technical term, defined for someone new to a field. Consider photosynthesis or an electron microscope defined for a first-year biology student; ohm or ampere defined for a tenth-grader in an electricity shop course; CPR or EKG for a nurse's aide. If you borrow information from a source, give credit to your source by mentioning it in the paragraph: write, for instance, "My textbook, *Introduction to Biology,* makes clear that photosynthesis involves. . . . "

9

Writing Persuasive Paragraphs

Defining Persuasive Writing

In persuasive writing you take a definite position and try to convince readers that they should agree with that position. You see persuasive writing on editorial pages of newspapers and in magazine columns. You hear persuasive writing in speeches on politics, religion, social issues, and other controversial topics.

Changing the beliefs of others is sometimes a long, difficult operation. Ideally, you will convince readers that they should agree with you. Generally, though, you are most likely to influence only those who are undecided. When readers have strong positions of their own—positions contrary to yours—the most you will accomplish is to get them to consider your views and to recognize that you have a reasonable viewpoint.

Perhaps the most familiar kind of persuasive writing is advertising. You know the purposes of advertising very well: to sell a product or service. You also know the principles that guide advertisers:

- know the market (the audience)
- get and hold attention
- convey a clear message in a memorable way
- keep the main message direct and relevant
- support that message with carefully selected, specific details
- leave a positive impression

Practice 9-1.   Examining persuasive writing in advertising

DIRECTIONS: *Find a newspaper or magazine advertisement that you be-lieve is well designed and attractive to readers. Answer these questions about that advertisement. Bring that advertisement (or a copy of it) to class.*

1. What did you see or read that stands out in your mind?

   _____

   _____

2. How did the advertisement get your attention?

   _____

3. What was the main message, stated briefly? _____

   _____

4. What details support that message? _____

   _____

5. In your opinion, what was especially persuasive in the wording or overall effect of this advertisement?

   _____

   _____

If you examine the advertisements you see regularly, you will find that some characteristics are fairly standard: most advertisements are brief, but they include some specific information; they get attention; and they convey a clear message.

As a writer, you face some of the advertiser's challenges and goals:

- understanding your audience
- getting and holding attention
- conveying a message in a clear, memorable way
- supporting that message with well-selected, specific information
- leaving a satisfying overall impression.

Though you can find some similarities between advertising and writ-ing persuasively, you will also find important *dis*similarities. As a writer, your work differs from that of advertisers in several ways:

- You normally have more complex ideas to express than "buy this product" or "use our services."
- You must go into greater detail to establish facts and reasons.
- You need well-worded prose, not catchy slogans.
- You cannot rely on repetition because your words will probably be read only once.

For all those reasons, *what* a persuasive paragraph says and *how* it says it must be more complex than what an ad says and how the copywriter says it.

For good examples of persuasive paragraphs, look at editorials in newspapers and opinion columns in magazines. In the best examples the writers support their positions with relevant facts, opinions of experts, details, and examples.

Practice 9-2.   Looking at persuasive writing in an editorial

DIRECTIONS: *Find an editorial on a topic that interests you. Answer the questions below. Bring the editorial (or a copy of it) to class.*

1. What is the source of this editorial?

   Source _____ Date _____

2. What is the main position in this editorial?

   _____

   _____

3. List two items of support (facts, opinions of experts, details, or examples)

   a. _____

   _____

   b. _____

   _____

4. Do you find this editorial persuasive? Why or why not?

   _____

   _____

   _____

As class discussion of Practice 9-2 will show, writers differ in their ways of trying to persuade their readers. Some approaches work better than others. As a writer, you must find and use approaches that will work, fitting the topic and the audience.

Using Techniques to Persuade

As a starting point in persuasive writing, apply the established principles of good paragraph writing:

- develop a narrow, workable topic
- focus attention on the topic idea
- provide concrete, relevant support
- organize in a logical way

Develop a Narrow, Workable Topic

To persuade others, you must narrow the topic so that you can focus on exactly the point you want to make. In this effort you can adopt the advertiser's strategy: target a message to a specific audience.

The first step toward shaping a workable topic is to select something you care about. You must believe in your position, and you must know a good deal about the issue. For instance, you may know of a specific problem at work, at school, or in the community. Because it affects you directly, you know about it, and you have strong feelings about it. As you think about this problem, a possible solution comes to mind. When writing, you can follow these steps:

1. Explain exactly what the problem is. You might point out the difficulties, inefficiencies, or hazards caused by the present situation.
2. Recommend a reasonable solution. Take into account the time, personnel, and money required.

A restaurant employee wrote this paragraph to her manager, explaining a problem and recommending two possible solutions:

[1]The dumpster behind our restaurant is not up to company specifications and needs immediate improvement. [2]Several families living nearby have complained that it is an eyesore. [3]They object to seeing it overflow, as it has on several occasions. [4]They also say it is a health hazard, especially for the children who might be playing nearby. [5]I have seen the

dumpster overflow, too, even though we try to keep the trash pushed inside it. ⁶Our dumpster is simply too small to hold all the refuse, so that we need the trash removed more than just twice a week. ⁷The problem can easily be solved by getting a larger dumpster or having more frequent pickups or both. ⁸The neighbors would no longer be upset, and employees would have an easier time keeping the back of the restaurant looking good.

Practice 9-3. Analyzing a persuasive paragraph about a work-related situation

DIRECTIONS: *Answer these questions about the paragraph above.*

1. In which sentences does the writer state the problem?

_____

2. In which sentences does she recommend solutions?

_____

3. Which sentence serves as the topic sentence? _____

_____

4. How do you know that the writer has first-hand knowledge about the

problem? _____

_____

5. The writer ties some of the suggestions in the "solution" part of the paragraph to statements made in the "problem" part. One example is the reference to the neighbors. What other examples can you find?

_____

_____

As a writer, you will find that persuasive writing often grows out of your experiences. You run into problems that cause inconvenience or annoyance, just as the writer of the paragraph preceding Practice 9-3 did.

The problems may cost time or money, or they may pose danger to health or safety. In one way or another, they cause worry that prompts you to write, explaining the problem and suggesting solutions. By writing to those who can change the situation, you might bring about change.

At other times, you might write about problems that do not affect you personally. Even so, you are well aware that something needs to be changed. Then you might address your audience as this student did:

[1]Your palms sweat. [2]Your face feels tight. [3]You smile and nod agreeably, trying hard to look interested in the conversation, but you'd rather be somewhere else. [4]The occasion could be a job interview or a blind date. [5]Worse yet, you might be talking with an amputee, a paraplegic, or a victim of cerebral palsy. [6]The fact is that most of us are uncomfortable around those who are disabled or disfigured. [7]Not only that, we feel uncomfortable about feeling uncomfortable. [8]So we smile more than usual and behave too agreeably. [9]These actions make us feel better, but they do not allow the normal give and take that all people need. [10]To overcome our feelings of self-consciousness, it helps to work with disadvantaged people in a setting where their abilities, not disabilities, show through. [11]Examples are summer camps, art and craft centers, and computer and biology workshops. [12]By seeing what can be done and sharing ideas and activities, we develop a more natural relationship with others. [13]The key to feeling comfortable with the disabled individual is to find that as human beings, we share interests, wants, and needs. [14]When we see people as individuals, we can start building real relationships.

Practice 9-4. Analyzing a persuasive paragraph about interpersonal relationships

DIRECTIONS: *Answer these questions about the paragraph above.*

1. What purpose is served by sentences 1, 2, and 3? _____

_____

2. Which sentence states the problem being discussed? _____

_____

3. Which sentences suggest solutions? _____

4. It can be argued that this student writer had too large a topic for a good paragraph. Do you agree or disagree and why? _____

   _____

5. It might be said that the student had a strong opening to the paragraph and a weak ending. Do you agree or disagree, and why? _____

   _____

6. Which sentences are broad and general? _____

7. Which sentences give specific details or examples? _____

   _____

8. In your opinion, has the writer provided an appropriate balance between general and specific statements?

   _____

   _____

In the two paragraphs above, the writers describe specific situations so that readers can understand those situations. Then the writers point out the need for change and suggest specific actions, such as putting a larger dumpster behind a restaurant and working with disabled people at camps and workshops.

Focus Attention on the Topic Idea

In persuasive writing, a strong topic sentence is even more important than it is elsewhere. To get readers to agree with you, they must understand exactly what point you are making.

In persuasive writing—unlike some other kinds of paragraph writing—you may be better off to begin with a statement *other than* the topic idea. You might entice the reader into the paragraph first with a statement that arouses interest and leads into the topic. After you have the reader's attention, you can move toward the topic idea.

You saw that strategy used by the student who wrote on the typical person's uneasiness when dealing with the disabled. The opening arouses curiosity. Readers wonder what the situation is that causes such a reaction:

> [1]Your palms sweat. [2]Your face feels tight. [3]You smile and nod agreeably, trying hard to look interested in the conversation, but you'd rather be somewhere else.

Then the writer mentions situations in which those reactions are possible:

> [4]The occasion could be a job interview or a blind date. [5]Worse yet, you might be talking with an amputee, a paraplegic, or a victim of cerebral palsy.

Finally, in the sixth sentence, the writer gets to the main idea in the paragraph: most of us are uncomfortable around those who are disabled or disfigured.

In the example below, an editorial writer begins with a startling statement that attracts attention. Then, gradually, this writer prepares readers for the topic idea that appears in the last sentence of the paragraph:

> [1]Africa is becoming a vast elephant graveyard. [2]Despite efforts to curtail the illegal ivory trade, elephants are falling by the hundreds each month to poachers who make a grisly living selling their tusks. [3]In just the past decade, the African elephant population has been cut in half, to less than 750,000; in another decade or two, the elephant could be gone. [4]Halfway measures to protect them have not even slowed the slaughter. [5]When member nations of the Convention on International Trade in Endangered Species (CITES) meet in October, they should ban all trade in ivory and be prepared to do whatever is necessary to enforce it.[*]

[*]*Minneapolis Star Tribune* (August 1, 1989), 8A.

Practice 9-5.   Comparing techniques of editorial writers

DIRECTIONS: *Look again at the editorial you used in Practice 9-2. Com-pare the opening paragraph of that editorial with the paragraph above.*

1. What is the topic idea in the paragraph above? _____

_____

2. What is the topic idea in the editorial you used in Practice 9-2? _____

_____

3. In the editorial you used in Practice 9-2, how did the editorial writer get

the reader's attention at the beginning? _____

4. In the editorial you used in Practice 9-2, how far did you read before you

came to the writer's position? _____

5. Which opening paragraph is more effective in getting the reader's atten-tion and leading to the topic idea, the paragraph above or the para-graph you used in Practice 9-2?

_____

Why? _____

_____

Provide Concrete, Relevant Support

To persuade others, you need exact information and reasons, and you must stay on the topic. Vague, rambling, overly general statements do not persuade readers.

Suppose you were a member of your city council. A citizen might write to request your help in getting a stop sign on a dangerous corner. Look at two versions of a paragraph that person might write. Then consider which one you would find more persuasive:

Paragraph A

[1]You'd better put a stop sign on the corner of First Street and Logan Avenue. [2]We are taxpayers, too, you know, and we deserve a sign there

because it is a busy corner and lots of accidents happen there. [3]Besides that, I am a voter, and I will not vote for you unless you serve our interests better. [4]I saw you on television, talking about traffic control, but what about our corner?

Paragraph B

[1]We need your help in getting a stop sign on the corner of First Street and Logan Avenue. [2]This corner is in a residential area, but lots of business traffic passes through, headed to the mall six blocks away. [3]In the past year, five serious accidents have occurred at that corner. [4]Three of them involved children crossing the street to get to school. [5]A ten-year-old boy spent three weeks in the hospital after being hit. [6]Two cars were totaled in those five accidents, so you know that property damage is serious, but danger to the children is the gravest worry.

Practice 9-6.   Looking for specific, relevant support

DIRECTIONS: *Answer these questions about the paragraphs above.*

1. In which paragraph does the writer offer evidence that the street is

   busy? _____

   What evidence is offered in that paragraph? _____

   _____

2. In which paragraph does the writer offer evidence to support the idea

   that "lots of accidents" occur? _____

   What evidence is offered in that paragraph? _____

   _____

3. The writer realizes that the sheer number of accidents is not all that matters. In Paragraph B, which sentences show the reader that the corner is dangerous as measured by more than the number of accidents?

   _____

4. Paragraph B is longer, but it covers less territory than Paragraph A. For instance, Paragraph B says nothing about the writer's being a voter or taxpayer. Even so, Paragraph B is much more convincing. Why?

_____

_____

Convincing support can take many forms. It can be factual, as you saw in the editorial on elephants and ivory. Quotations from experts or reliable witnesses will support a position, as will examples and reasons.

In most instances, writers draw upon several kinds of supporting evidence. To keep a paragraph reasonably brief, some statements are rather general; they summarize information that could be discussed at length.

Look again at sentences 2 and 4 in that paragraph:

> [1]Africa is becoming a vast elephant graveyard. [2]Despite efforts to curtail the illegal ivory trade, elephants are falling by the hundreds each month to poachers who make a grisly living selling their tusks. [3]In just the past decade, the African elephant population has been cut in half, to less than 750,000; in another decade or two, the elephant could be gone. [4]Halfway measures to protect them have not even slowed the slaughter. [5]When member nations of the Convention on International Trade in Endangered Species (CITES) meet in October, they should ban all trade in ivory and be prepared to do whatever is necessary to enforce it.

Sentence 2 gives the reason elephants are endangered; sentence 4 lets us know that past efforts to stop the slaughter have done little good. Facts are included in the paragraph, too, as we see in sentence 3.

As a general rule, you will be more persuasive if you use a few well-chosen, significant facts and reasons rather than many weak or mediocre ones. Quality is more important than quantity. Remember, too, that readers find a recital of facts and statistics dreary and mind boggling. On the other hand, well-chosen facts can make the situation clear. As you saw in the example above, the editorial writer gracefully weaves facts into the paragraph in sentence 3, using just enough factual information to support the main idea.

Organize in a Logical Way

For persuasive writing, you can use any pattern discussed in this book. You can combine patterns as you think best. The best advice about organization—perhaps the only worthwhile advice—you have seen many times in other chapters: arrange your sentences to help readers understand and follow your ideas easily.

Though many patterns of organization are possible, perhaps the most used for persuasive writing are these:

- moving from the least important to the most important facts and reasons
- showing contrasts between what is and what should be
- showing effects if a present "cause" or situation is not changed

To see what can be done with these patterns used in combination, consider this sample paragraph:

[1]Recently the school board proposed cutting out extracurricular activities at Middletown High School. [2]Though I realize that money has to be saved somehow, this proposal will cost more than it saves, for both the students and the community. [3]In the past, many students have worked and studied hard enough to earn scholarships for college. [4]But if programs are cut back, for instance, in sports and music, today's students won't have records to show colleges, so that they will lose their chance at scholarship money. [5]One board member did say, "We'll let some students transfer into a different school to participate if they need to build records." [6] No one dared, however, to estimate the cost of those transfers. [7]Money would probably not be saved, but lost. [8]No one has talked about the loss of revenue brought in from the community if activities are eliminated. [9]Money will be lost because of lost sales in ticket offices and at refreshment stands. [10]If community spirit, created in part by pride in the school's teams, starts to diminish, taxpayers may take less interest in supporting the schools. [11]The long-term effects need to be considered, not just the budget on the table at this moment. [12]If the school board will take a longer look at this proposal, the hidden costs may well kill the proposal.

Practice 9-7. Examining the organization of a persuasive paragraph

DIRECTIONS: *Answer these questions about the paragraph above.*

1. Which sentence states the topic idea? _____

2. Which sentences use comparison/contrast (past vs. present situations, for

   instance)? _____

3. The writer arranges arguments against the proposal, starting with the immediate and ending with future effects. In which sentences are these effects mentioned? _____

   _____

4. The writer deals with probable effects that will develop out of the "cause," the cutting of extracurricular activities. Which sentences cite specific effects? _____

   _____

5. The writer did not mention that students learn a great deal from extra-curricular activities. Can you explain why such an important point was left out? _____

   _____

   The main thing to remember about organization is that it must help readers understand the point being made. If you take your readers into account, then consider your topic and the supporting information, you will be ready to adopt the patterns that seem appropriate.

   When you write to persuade, you also need to remember these two final points:

   - Be moderate, restrained, and polite even when you are angry or upset. A moderate, reasonable tone is more effective because it appeals to readers; it does not put them on the defensive.
   - Watch the logic of your statements. Fallacies of reasoning that sometimes creep into attempts at persuasion get in the way and distract readers.

Here is a summary of common fallacies:

1. Hasty generalizing or generalizing from a single example. In this fallacy, the writer makes a broad, inclusive statement that cannot be supported.

   Poor: All politicians are crooks.
              or
              Our fire chief was convicted of taking kickbacks from insurance companies, showing that our city officials are dishonest.
   Better: When our fire chief was convicted of taking kickbacks from insurance companies in arson cases, we realized how important honesty is for elected officials.

2. Begging the question (also called "circular reasoning") means saying something is so because it is so.

   Poor: Our city is losing population because fewer people live here now than ten years ago.
              or
              Two large manufacturing plants moved out of this city because they relocated to another state.
   Better: Our city lost population over the past ten years because two large manufacturing plants moved out, causing 1,850 workers to relocate.

3. *Non sequitur,* meaning literally, it does not follow. With a non sequitur, there is no logical connection between the premise and the conclusion.

   Poor: In the last year, five serious accidents have occurred on the dangerous corner of First Street and Logan Avenue. Just last week, the city put a stop sign at Second Street and Maxwell Avenue.
              or
              A stop sign lets children cross safely because it stops traffic.
   Better: In the last year, five serious accidents have occurred on the dangerous corner of First Street and Logan Avenue. The city should put a stop sign on that corner so that children can cross the street safely.

4. *Ad hominem,* meaning attacking the person, not the issue. Whether the reader or some third person is attacked, the effect is equally poor.

   Poor: (addressed to a city council member):
              When you ran for election, you talked a lot about keeping children safe on our streets. Then the minute you got elected, all you did was vote for a raise for yourself and the rest of the council. All you do is think of yourself.
              or

(addressed to newspaper readers, about city council members):

Our council members look out for themselves and no one else. All they think about is their salaries and reelection. They are nothing but lazy, selfish people who don't care a thing about voters once they are elected.

Better: We need a stop sign on the dangerous corner of First Street and Logan Avenue. In the last year, five serious accidents have occurred there. One of those accidents killed a ten-year-old boy, and another accident crippled a seven-year-old girl for life.

5. *Post hoc ergo propter hoc* (usually referred to as post hoc), meaning literally *after this, therefore because of this.* Two ideas are involved: one is a "cause" or a premise, and the other is an "effect." Cause and effect are confused in that there may actually be no cause-effect connection between the two ideas.

Poor: I got a new hairstyle last week, and right away it paid off because my boss gave me a raise.

or

My brother-in-law sat down at the dinner table, and California suffered its worst earthquake in decades.

Better: I got a new hairstyle last week. Another recent change was my unexpected raise in pay, effective last Friday.

My mother-in-law was sitting down at the dinner table when we all heard about California's earthquake.

Practice 9-8.   Evaluating the tone and logic in a paragraph

DIRECTIONS: *As the manager of a discount department store, you received this paragraph from one of your employees. Read the paragraph, keeping in mind that the writer is a capable cashier, not a troublemaker. Then answer the questions below:*

[1]I am being paid $5 per hour, and I am never one to complain. [2]In fact, I'm glad to have this job. [3]But yesterday I saw a sign at the restaurant across the street. [4]It was an advertisement for dishwashers at $5 per hour. [5]Why should I work for only $5 an hour after ten months on this job if a newcomer can start over there at the same rate? [6]I am a hard worker. [7]By the time taxes are withheld, I end up with a lot less than $5 an hour. [8]My job is more responsible than the job advertised at that greasy-spoon joint across the street. [9]If you were alert to the labor market, you'd see that I deserve a raise. [10]I'm probably not the only one around here who does..

1. In which sentences is the writer vague, rambling, and overly general?

   _____

2. In which sentences does the writer beg the question or use non

   sequiturs? _____

3. In which sentences does the writer use an inappropriate tone?

   _____

4. Besides the faults specifically cited in questions 1, 2, and 3, what else do

   you find objectionable in this paragraph? _____

   _____

5. Do you find anything contradictory in the writer's statements?

   _____

   As the examples in this chapter show, you need a clear statement of your position, solid evidence to support that position, and an appropriate tone or attitude in your writing. You must have a definite viewpoint in mind, and you must express that position so clearly that the reader knows exactly where you stand. To convince the reader, you need valid reasons and sufficient, relevant evidence in support of your position. You must stick to the topic, or your reader will be distracted, just as the reader of the paragraph in Practice 9-8 would be. Finally, by using a moderate, reasonable tone, you will win respect for your views. If you keep these basic principles in mind, you can present your views effectively.

Summary

- Persuasive writing is designed to persuade readers to accept a particular point of view.
- To be persuasive, develop a narrow, workable topic; focus attention on the topic idea; provide concrete, relevant support; and organize in a logical way.
- Vague, rambling, and overly general statements do not persuade readers, nor do errors in logic, such as hasty generalization, begging the question, non sequitur, ad hominem, or the post hoc fallacy.
- Begging the question means saying the same thing twice: it amounts to saying that something is so because it is so.

- Non sequitur means "it does not follow"; that is, the conclusion does not follow from the premises.

- Ad hominem means attacking the person, rather than addressing the issue.

- In most cases, persuasive paragraphs include several kinds of support. Writers can also combine methods of organization in persuasive writing.

Exercise 9-1:   Examining persuasive writing in editorials or opinion columns

DIRECTIONS: *Find two editorials in newspapers or opinion columns in magazines. Use passages on the same topic (taxes, public safety, the environment, education, political candidates, or another current issue). Answer the questions below. Bring the articles (or copies of them) to class for class discussion.*

1. What are the sources of these two editorials or columns?

   a. Source _____

       Date _____

   b. Source _____

       Date _____

2. What are the main positions in these editorials or columns?

   a. _____

   _____

   b. _____

   _____

3. Name two ways in which the writers agree.

   a. _____

   _____

   b. _____

   _____

4. Name two ways in which the writers disagree.

   a. _____

   _____

   b. _____

   _____

5. Find one sentence that strikes you as particularly appropriate or convincing. What is that statement? (summarize or quote exactly)

   Source: _____

   Sentence: _____

   _____

   _____

   _____

6. Consider the sentence you cited in answer 5. What made that sentence stand out? (Is it especially well worded? Does it give you a significant detail or fact? Does it form a striking beginning or ending? Or what?)

   _____

   _____

   _____

   _____

7. Which editorial or column is more persuasive? Why?

   _____

   _____

   _____

   _____

   _____

Exercise 9-2: Revising faulty statements

DIRECTIONS: *The statements below are faulty in their logic. You will find examples of these kinds of faulty logic:*

- *hasty generalization or generalizing from a single example*
- *begging the question (circular reasoning)*
- *non sequitur (it does not follow)*
- *ad hominem (attacking the person, not the issue)*
- *post hoc (suggesting a cause-effect relationship where none exists)*

First, explain what is wrong in each example. Sometimes you may find more than one fallacy. Second, revise the example to make it logical. Invent details if you need them.

Example

Statements: You are not allowed to register for that class until next month. The class is already closed, however.

Problem: Non sequitur because the second statement does not follow from the first. The second statement is irrelevant. In fact, there is no logical connection at all.

Revision: Even if the class weren't already closed, which it is, you and other freshmen could not register for it until next month.

1. The team has won the last three games, all of them home games. Teams play better when playing at home.

Problem: _____

Revision: _____

_____

2. Our team can't win any games because our opponents always win.

Problem: _____

Revision: _____

_____

3. Your political party got into office last year, and more people moved out of the city in the next ten months than at any other time in a decade. Now you can see what happens when that party gets elected.

   Problem: _____

   Revision: _____ ˡ ___

   _____

4. The Babylonian army was outnumbered by the Assyrians because the Assyrians had more troops.

   Problem: _____

   Revision: _____

   _____

5. Hurry up and order our new recliners today! We will begin placing orders in two or three weeks.

   Problem: _____

   Revision: _____

   _____

6. I know exactly why we're losing: that coach is lazy and dumb. All he cares about is his salary for next year and gaining yardage on the cheerleaders.

   Problem: _____

   Revision: _____

   _____

7. There are so many things to complain of in life that I can't decide which one to discuss, so I'll mention a couple of them.

   Problem: _____

   Revision: _____

   _____

8. Fast food places are more numerous now than ever before. It must be a Communist plot.

   Problem: _____

   Revision: _____

   _____

9. I saw that can of gasoline explode. It was a hazard that I could foresee, because gasoline is explosive.

   Problem: _____

   Revision: _____

   _____

10. I know why this restaurant is losing money! That new busboy is always snacking at the buffet counter.

    Problem: _____

    Revision: _____

    _____

Exercise 9-3: Analyzing persuasive paragraphs

Directions: *Analyze each of the paragraphs below, considering how persuasive they are. To guide your analysis, answer the questions that follow them.*

Paragraph 1

¹My anger lies with those lazy people who are supposed to take care of Woodrow Wilson Park. ²This park is used a lot by adults and children, but the littering has become a big problem. ³The broken beer bottles and empty fast-food containers on the ground prevent us, the hardworking citizens, from walking barefoot in the grass. ⁴The litter also makes the park look like a dumping ground. ⁵I feel that as adults, we are all responsible for picking up after ourselves, and also, if we see other trash, we

should take the few extra moments and pick it up. [6]The city has provided trash bins in all the parks, so there is no excuse for littering. [7]The city also put up signs that promote keeping our parks clean, but evidently many people pay no attention to cans or signs. [8]If those in charge of the parks want to control littering, they are going to have to patrol and impose fines on those who leave messes. [9]It looks like the police ought to be more alert to the activities going on in the park. [10]The broken beer bottles mean that people are drinking there, and drinking is supposedly prohibited in the park. [11]It could be that underage drinkers are using the park. [12]Where is law enforcement? [13]If those in charge will not live up to their responsibilities, our parks will soon be unfit for anyone, and a real loss to the community, but especially to the children.

1. What is the main idea? _____

   _____

2. Which sentences give facts and reasons that support the main idea?

   _____

   _____

3. In which sentences do you find the writer begging the question or using

   non sequiturs? _____

4. In which sentences do you find irrelevant details?

   _____

5. Do you feel that the tone is inappropriate? If so, in which sentences?

   _____

6. Do you find this paragraph persuasive? Why or why not?

   _____

   _____

   _____

Paragraph 2

[1]Until last August, I never gave much thought to the skill of swimming. [2]I took swimming for granted because I learned young and so did

all my friends. ³On that August day I suddenly was convinced that everyone should be taught to swim—and taught when very young. ⁴What convinced me was the scare I got over my two-year-old cousin Derek. ⁵He was visiting us and playing in our back yard. ⁶We have a pool, so my mother and I were watching him in case he got into any trouble. ⁷I had gone inside the house to get something to drink when I heard my mother screaming for me to come out. ⁸As I came running out, I could see that Derek had fallen into the pool. ⁹My mother can't swim, so I jumped in after him with my shoes and all. ¹⁰When I reached him, I grabbed him and pulled him to the side of the pool. ¹¹Luckily he was okay, except for being plenty scared. ¹²But what if I hadn't been there? ¹³What if I had not known how to swim? ¹⁴Since that day I've taught Derek how to swim. ¹⁵Still, whenever I see a child playing by water, I am very uneasy. ¹⁶I know that some people have a "take it or leave it" attitude about swimming, but I feel that every child must be taught how to swim.

1. Which sentences state the writer's position? _____

2. In your opinion, would the paragraph have been more or less persuasive

   if the writer had given statistics about drowning accidents? _____

   Why? _____

   _____

3. Are any of the statements irrelevant or overly general? _____

4. Besides the chronological pattern in the narrative, do you find other

   organizational patterns here? _____

5. Do you find this paragraph persuasive? Why or why not? _____

   _____

   _____

Paragraph 3

¹The time standards set by the main office are unfair for those of us who operate the machines. ²These standards are all but impossible to make. ³I know that managers want to cut costs, but these ridiculous

standards are not the way to do it. ⁴There are many ways to cut costs, and you should try those ways first. ⁵Right now we have old machines that need to be replaced or rebuilt and updated. ⁶It would be more sensible in the long run to get better equipment. ⁷Then maybe we could meet the time standards, or at least get a little closer. ⁸To cut costs, it would be smart to get rid of unneeded employees. ⁹Some departments I know have too many people for the work that needs to be done. ¹⁰Instead of expecting the impossible from machine operators, why not clean up the act around here?

1. This paragraph seems to state a problem and suggest solutions, giving it some sense of purpose and overall a sense of order. Which sentences deal with a problem?

   _____

   Which sentences deal with solutions? _____

2. As a reader, you may feel that a lot of necessary information is missing. For instance, you might like to know to whom this paragraph is addressed (to which audience). What other information would you need in order to understand what the writer means? _____

   _____

   _____

   _____

3. This paragraph is not persuasive for several obvious reasons. List two of those reasons. Point to specific sentences as examples of weak points, if you wish.

   a. _____

   _____

   _____

   b. _____

   _____

   _____

Exercise 9-4:   Writing a persuasive paragraph

DIRECTIONS: *Write a persuasive paragraph on a topic of your choice. See if you can make it a model of good persuasive writing: direct, focused, narrow, and powerful. Naturally you will avoid the many weaknesses you found in the sample paragraphs in Exercise 9-3.*

Consider mailing a finished copy to the editor of a newspaper, a city council member, a state legislator, or any other person who might influence change.

Suggestions for Finding Topics:

Think of a problem you deal with directly, perhaps one of these:

- traffic congestion at a particular corner
- parking at school, work, or elsewhere
- a bus that often runs late
- a coworker whose conduct on the job causes frustration
- a troublemaking customer you see often
- a school or on-the-job requirement or rule that you find silly or objectionable

Think of a problem in your community at large, perhaps one of these:

- pollution in a specific lake or creek
- the need for traffic signals at a certain intersection
- the need for more jogging paths, parks, playgrounds, or other public facilities
- the need to get rid of a certain building, to remodel it for better use, or to preserve it for historical reasons

Do not write an ad for a product or service. Do not write on huge problems like the federal debt or acid rain or destruction of the rain forests or any other national or international issue. Limit yourself to local issues or your own day-to-day problems.

10

Revising and Proofreading

The last two steps in the writing process are revising and proofreading, functions that are sometimes confused. Actually, they refer to very different things:

- Revising means improving the **content** of your writing. When you revise, you look—carefully and critically—to see exactly what you have written. Then you change and improve the content.
- Proofreading means improving the **form** of your writing. When you proofread, you check all the surface features, such as spelling, grammar, capitalization, and punctuation. If you find errors in these and similar features, you repair them.

Many times, you improve both content and form in the same reading. As you work on each draft of your paper, you should improve anything that needs improvement. Fix it right then, the moment you see the need. But later, as you are finishing your paper, make a deliberate effort to revise thoroughly, then proofread. This chapter gives you specific guidance in both these steps.

Revising to Serve Audience and Purpose

Before you can revise and proofread, you must remember your readers and your purpose for writing. You might want to write to a friend or relative for your own private reasons, or you might have to write for work or school. Of course, you have to think about the topic, the main idea,

support, coherence, and organization. Certainly, all the while, you must remember the goal: to communicate with your audience and serve a chosen
purpose.

The words "audience" and "reader" are used over and over in this
book because no matter what you write—or when or where—you must
think about the people with whom you are communicating. Would you
pick up a telephone and talk to the dial tone? Probably not. Likewise, it
makes no sense to pick up a pen and start writing to the paper or sit at a
word processor and write to the screen. The words on paper or on a screen
are on their way to readers, your audience.

You write for the same reason that you talk, simply to share ideas with
others. Writing must be more polished, more carefully thought out than
talking, but the goal is the same. In both cases, a message is conveyed to a
receiver (an audience), and the message has a purpose.

To get a better sense of audience and purpose, think of yourself as a
part of an audience, as well as a writer with messages to communicate. As a
reader, you receive purposeful messages from others, and in turn, you often reply with messages of your own.

Practice 10-1.   Thinking about getting and sending messages

DIRECTIONS: *Think about situations in which you have communicated recently. Then answer these questions:*

1. What written communication have you received in the past week (at
   home and at work)? A possible list has been started; add items, and subtract those which don't belong.

   a letter from _____

   a bill from _____

   an assignment sheet from _____

   junk-mail ads from _____

   a renewal notice from _____

   a memo from _____

   _____

   _____

2. About how many written messages have you received in the past

   week? _____

   About how many will you respond to, in writing? _____

3. What written communication have you sent out in the past week (at home and at work)? A possible list has been started; add items, and subtract those which don't belong.

   a letter to _____

   a bill to _____

   an offer to sell (or ads) _____

   a school assignment for _____

   a memo to _____

   a report or proposal to _____

   _____

   _____

4. About how many written messages have you sent out in the past

   week? _____

   About how many written responses do you expect? _____

   Practice 10-1 reminds you of your roles in communication with others. As a reader of the other people's ideas, you are part of various audiences—some at home, others at work or school, and others in your community. You respond to those ideas in different ways, depending upon who has written to you and what purpose that person had in mind.

   As a writer, you want to communicate with your readers. To do so, you must consider your readers' reactions. Though it is difficult to do, try to see your statements as the readers will see them. It helps to anticipate the questions readers might ask, such as these:

   - What is the main idea?
   - What makes you think so? or How do you know?
   - What evidence supports that idea?
   - What difference does it make?

If you express your ideas clearly, with adequate support, readers will understand your purpose and your message.

To reach that goal, you must revise. In other words, you must examine your writing *critically,* then change and improve it. Revising literally means "re-seeing" or "seeing again." When you revise, you see your statements again. You think about your ideas critically, questioning whether you have expressed them in the best ways possible. The "best" ways are the clearest, most exact, most easily understood by readers.

While revising, you might make one or more of these changes:

- narrow the main idea still more
- add more supporting information to explain the main idea more fully
- replace overly general statements with specific ones
- throw out irrelevant statements
- add stronger, more relevant details, examples, facts, or quotations
- build connecting links between statements to show relationships of ideas
- rearrange the statements for a more logical order
- create a more appropriate beginning or ending or both

In revising, you can make as many changes as you want or need. In determining which changes to make, you are guided by your awareness of the reader's needs and by your knowledge of paragraph writing.

When revising, draw upon all your knowledge of paragraphs and your experience with writing them. In previous chapters, you learned that your first attempts at writing should be free and flowing. As you think about your topic, you narrow the scope. Then you develop a topic sentence, support, coherence, and organization. In short, you have learned the principles that underlie paragraph writing; consequently, you know what to look for as you revise your paragraphs.

No one can tell you exactly how much revising a piece of writing needs because no one can tell you exactly what you should say or how you should say it. You are the only judge because you know to whom you are writing, why you are writing, and what you mean to say when you write. No one else has exactly your knowledge or insight. Most of all, no one else has your personality, and your personality comes through in your writing.

In other words, the burden—or responsibility—is upon you. The previous chapters have helped you know what to look for. Now, for your convenience, here is a set of questions you can apply to your paragraphs or to paragraphs written by others:

A Checklist for Revising Paragraphs

Main idea: *The paragraph must focus upon one clear main idea.*

Does the paragraph focus on one main idea?
Is the main idea narrow enough to be managed in one paragraph?

Topic sentence (T.S.):   *The T.S. announces the topic and limits the scope of that topic.*

Does the T.S. limit the scope sufficiently so that the topic idea is manageable in one paragraph?

Is the T.S. well worded and exact, not vague and overly general?

Does the T.S. go beyond facts, expressing an attitude or opinion?

If the T.S. is factual, does it state a fact that requires explanation in the paragraph?

Is the T.S. a complete thought, expressing one dominant idea (not two or more)?

Development: *A well-developed paragraph provides enough relevant information so that readers get a clear, accurate impression.*

Do all other sentences support the idea stated in the T.S.?

Do readers get enough information to explain the main idea?

Does the information appear to be accurate?

If quotations are used, are they appropriate and helpful? Does the writer give credit to the source?

Is the information specific?

Is every sentence relevant?

Coherence: *In a coherent paragraph, all the sentences are smoothly connected to all the others and relationships among ideas are clear.*

Do the sentences flow smoothly from one to another in logical order?

Are transitional words and phrases used to make the connections between ideas clear?

Are key words and phrases repeated to connect statements to the topic idea?

Does every sentence belong in the paragraph?

Organization: *The statements should be arranged in some logical, orderly way—not haphazardly.*

Does the paragraph have a sense of order?

What pattern(s) of organization does the writer use? Are those patterns appropriate for this material?

Do the main supporting points stand out clearly?

Are those main supporting points arranged in some logical way?

Does the paragraph have a suitable ending?

Awareness of audience: *The paragraph should answer questions that would naturally occur to readers.*

What do readers want or need to know?
When? Where? Why? How? What happened later? How did this turn out?
What difference does it make?

All the items in this list contribute to making a good paragraph. When you revise, look at your paper with these questions in mind. If you have remembered all these points and if you handled them well, you will probably communicate well with readers.

Proofreading for Accuracy

After you have revised your ideas, you are ready for the last steps in the writing process. One of those steps is proofreading; the other is preparing your paper in proper manuscript form. Proofreading means checking each word, sentence, capital letter, and punctuation mark to be sure each item is exactly right. When it is, you can prepare a copy of your paragraph, using the manuscript form outlined in Appendix A, page 249.

When you proofread, you may find any of these items:

- misspelled or mistyped words
- inappropriate word choice
- unnecessary punctuation marks
- places that need punctuation
- unnecessary capital letters
- places that need capital letters
- abbreviations that should be replaced with complete words
- numerals where words should be used
- faulty grammar (often of verbs or pronouns)
- inconsistency with singular and plural forms
- sentence errors

You might find a mixture of these items. What you find doesn't matter; what matters is that you find and repair your errors.

Proofreading is a bit easier if you read with a colored pen in hand and mark anything questionable while you go through your paper. Then go back and check on individual items.

For instance, as a student was preparing a response to Practice 8-6, he wrote a draft of the paragraph below. Then he marked his paper as shown

here. He fixed each item before typing the final copy. The symbols he used
are found in Appendix B, pages 250–252.

punct

[1]To fail your driving test you must
do everything just right. [2]First you must
make sure to insult the examiner whose *sp*
giving the test. [3]You could comment on
the way he is dressed, or make fun of any
punct
disfigurement he might have. [4]When preparing to start the test make sure the seat-
punct
belt is tucked into the seat or behind

cs where it will be out of the way, then you
can move around easily in the car.

cs [5]Starting the car, make sure to rev the
motor up, this cleans it out and shows the

cs exminer whose in charge. [6]Place only one
sp
hand on the stearing wheel, that way your
sp
other hand is free to adjust the radio or
hold your cigaratte. [7]When pulling away
sp
from the curb, glance into the mirror for
cars. [8]Don't look over your sholder be-
sp
cause you might hit the car ahead of you.
[9]Drive at least the speed limit if not faster *punct*

shift tense so you never held up traffic. [10]If you're
on a two lane road don't signal lane
punct
changes becuase it will let another driver *shift agr.*
sp
know what you want to do and they might
cut you off. [11]At intersections, be sure
sp
you have enough speed to get through
before the light changes. [12]No matter how *frag.*
close another car might be. [13]Then when
sp   *sp*
you parellel park, remember to knock all the

cs cones down, stop far enough from the
curb so your door won't hit it. [14]If you follow all these steps, you will be sure to fail
your driving test.

Practice 10-2. Examining a student's proofreading

DIRECTIONS: *Answer these questions about the paragraph above.*

1. Which words seem to be mistyped, as opposed to misspelled? How can you tell? _____

   _____

2. How does the statement marked "frag" differ from the ones marked "CS"? (To review the concepts, see Appendix B, page 250.) _____

   _____

3. After repairing the items marked, the student had a paragraph with specific strengths. Name three good characteristics of this paragraph. (Rely on your knowledge of paragraphing, and refer to the checklist for revising.)

   a. _____

   b. _____

   c. _____

Proofreading is hard work, and it takes time. One reason it is hard is that you know what your writing is supposed to say. After all, you have worked over the ideas—planning, drafting, and revising them. It is only natural to see what you expect to see.

To help you see what is actually present on the paper, try these devices:

1. If possible, allow some time to pass between writing, revising, and proofreading. The passing of time will put some distance between you and your writing. You will see your statements anew, more nearly as your readers will.
2. Read your work slowly, out loud. Listen to each word and each sentence. You might discover that some passages do not sound right; if so, you will know that you need to fix something.
3. Read slowly, preferably out loud, but start at the end and read sentence by sentence, from the last sentence to the first. Because reading sentences in reverse order destroys the flow of ideas, you are forced to

consider sentences individually. You will see what you wrote, not just what you meant to write.

4. Go through your work several times. Each time, check one feature; you might check your spelling in one reading and verb tenses in another. Set aside one reading to examine each sentence, making sure that you have no fragments or run-on sentences.

As you proofread, you will find an up-to-date dictionary very helpful. Of course, it provides the correct spelling of words—though you may sometimes have to guess how a word starts in order to find it. The dictionary can help you distinguish between commonly confused words such as "affect" and "effect" or "accept" and "except." It will also point out synonyms and explain the distinctions between them. As you use the dictionary, you will discover new words or new meanings of familiar words. For all these reasons, the dictionary is a valuable tool.

If you have access to a spelling checker on a computer, you will find that device helpful, too, but you must understand its limitations. Unless that checker can examine words in context, it won't find all the mistyped or misspelled words. For instance, it will not flag "it" or "in" or "if" because all these words are properly spelled. If you have mistyped a letter in one of those words, the spelling checker will not catch the error.

You can use the checklist below as a convenient reminder of things to look for as you proofread. If you are not familiar with some of the terms in the list, consult grammar books or handbooks.

Checklist for Proofreading Paragraphs

Words

Is the spelling correct?

If the word is hyphenated, is that correct, or should it be spelled without the hyphen?

Is the word used in its proper context? Have commonly confused words been misused? (*to* vs. *too* or *its* vs. *it's,* for example)

If the word is plural, has the correct plural form been used?

If numbers are expressed, are words and numerals used in a logical and standard way?

If abbreviations are used, are their meanings clear?

If any abbreviation is unfamiliar, has the writer explained it in words?

Is the word choice exact, or would another word express the meaning better in some places?

Sentences

Is each sentence complete?
Does each complete thought end with proper punctuation?
If complete thoughts are put together into compound sentences, is the
    punctuation correct? (a semicolon or a comma plus a coordinating
    conjunction)
Do compound sentences join closely related thoughts, as they should?
Is parallelism used when appropriate?

Grammar

Do subjects and verbs agree—singular with singular, plural with plural?
Do pronouns and their antecedents agree in number (singular with sin-
    gular, plural with plural) and gender?
Is pronoun usage consistently in first, second, or third person?
Are the modifiers placed correctly—none dangling or misplaced?
Is the verb complete?
Is the verb tense logical and consistent?

Punctuation

If complete thoughts are joined with coordinating conjunctions (for, and,
    nor, but, or, yet, so), is a comma used before the conjunction?
If a semicolon is used, are there complete thoughts on each side of the
    semicolon?
If quotation marks, parentheses, or brackets are used, can you find both
    the left side and the right? (These marks are used in pairs.)
Have apostrophes been used properly to show possession and to indicate
    contractions?
Are titles of books, magazines, and newspapers italicized or underlined?

Capitalization

Are proper nouns and words derived from proper nouns capitalized?
Have common nouns, like "high school," been left in lower case?
Have the words in titles been capitalized properly?

Obviously, not all the items on the checklist come up in every paragraph, but these items do come up frequently. From time to time, you will
need to consult reference books about special situations requiring other

punctuation marks or other special effects. Remember that close, careful reading is essential whenever you write.

You can safely assume that good revising and proofreading of your school work will result in better grades. But the value of revising and proofreading goes far beyond grades. When you revise and proofread, you ensure better communication with readers, whoever and wherever they are. You eliminate distractions that would interfere with communicating ideas; your readers will not puzzle over your meaning, your spelling, or any other feature of your writing.

In short, revising ensures that you are saying well exactly what you want to say. Proofreading ensures that your ideas are presented in a credible way: it shows that you know how to present your ideas and that you care enough to present them well.

Summary

- The purpose of writing is to communicate ideas to readers, an audience that may not be seen or heard from, but is nonetheless present.

- Revising means seeing again, then changing statements so that readers will understand more easily, more precisely, and more fully.

- Revising means examining the main idea, the topic sentence, the supporting evidence, the coherence, and the organization of the paragraph.

- Revising provides a chance to sharpen the focus of the paragraph, change the order of ideas, evaluate the logic, and provide more or different supporting statements.

- Proofreading means looking critically at words, sentences, grammar, punctuation, and capitalization.

- Proofreading includes checking spellings and meanings of words, watching for commonly confused words, and considering other words that would better express the intended meaning.

- Proofreading requires examining sentences to be sure they are complete and correct. It also means checking subject/verb agreement, verb tense, pronoun choice, use of modifiers, and parallelism.

- Revising and proofreading ensure that readers understand exactly what is meant and that they can read without distractions.

Exercise 10-1:   Revising drafts for improved focus

DIRECTIONS: *Revise **any three** of these rough drafts so that they can be used as opening sentences for a paragraph. Invent details, if you wish, and reword any statements you find here. Give the statements focus so that paragraphs can be built upon them, adding further support.*
   Write on separate paper.

Examples

Original Version: The novel was quite boring to me. It had such a predictable plot, and the main characters were just stereotypes, almost stick figures, like on television.

Revision: The book *It* by Stephen King is too predictable to be interesting. For example, it was no surprise that a monster was going to come out of the gutter and eat the boy even before he started talking to the monster. There is no reason why a reader would be taken by surprise.

1. I will never forget how scared I was, walking down that street. I'm used to big cities, and I know that we have a lot of homeless people around. They don't frighten me, but the drug addicts do. So there I was, minding my own business and not thinking about the surroundings too much.

2. Democracy is the greatest system of government the world has ever seen, and it has seen a lot of systems. You take, for instance, the New England town meeting. People can come and listen, speak out, and vote on things that matter to them. In most places today there is no chance for people to speak out, let alone vote on issues.

3. Prejudice is not a thing that I paid any attention to until my family moved to a small town in the Midwest. No matter where I went in that town, I stood apart because no one else looked even the least bit Hispanic (nobody except the other people in my family). I had it hardest in some ways because I was in school, and I was at an awkward age anyhow, being only fourteen.

4. Shyness to me and what it can do. Shyness makes it hard to meet people, make friends, or enjoy new experiences. It can blind others to your strong points. It leads to feelings of depression, anxiety, and loneliness. It can prevent you from speaking up for your rights.

5. My best friend is Elaine. I could go on and on about our friendship, but we met in high school, and we've been close friends ever since. Some of

the things she has done for me are driving me to school, buying me a bracelet, and cooking dinner for me on my birthday. Some people just say, "Oh, ya, I've got a girlfriend," like it is nothing special. For me, Elaine is very special.

Exercise 10-2: Revising and proofreading paragraphs

DIRECTIONS: *The paragraphs below need revising and proofreading. Use the checklists in this chapter as reminders while you examine the paragraphs.*
Rewrite words and sentences. Invent specific information if you feel it is needed. Draw lines through irrelevant ideas. Write your corrections between the lines. The first lines of Paragraph 1 have been done as an example.

Paragraph 1

1	When the ~~deafaning~~ *deafening* noise of the ~~brake~~ *break* is heard, it
2	signals to everyone that one of my favorite games in the
3	world has begun. It's pool, ⁁ really great action-filled
4	game. I started playing at 11 and kept playing ever since.
5	Mostly at the poolhall around the corner from where I live.
6	You have to know the game to see how much skill it take.
7	The frist pool player whips their stick up and pokes the cue
8	ball with it, the cue ball hits another ball and that other
9	ball sinks, it has to sink otherwise it isn't their turn
10	anymore. Then if it isn't his turn anymore his opponent
11	gets the turn unless he doesn't have an opponent. If he
12	doesn't have an opponent than he will have too shoot again
13	anyways. If he can clear the table off with not too many
14	shoots then he is an alright pool player. I know because I
15	played alot, it takes skill and a whole lot of
16	concentration, still it is such a fast moving game that it
17	never gets boring.

Paragraph 2

1	The word friendship is hard for some people to explain
2	so they just brush off the word and say, Yes, she is just a
3	friend. They don't think much about what a true friend

4   means to a person. You have to respect your friends. With
5   a little more thought most people would realize that
6   friendship means a special relationship. An example is the
7   relationship between my girlfriend Janet and I. She is
8   special 'cause she always knew what I was thinking. We met
9   in 9th grade and ever since she has been special. Somebody
10   I could always count on. And somebody to share things with.
11   She did a lot of nice things for me, helping me shop, going
12   to the movies, amusement parks, and she worked on schoolwork
13   with me. Like any good friend, Janet would listen when I
14   had problems. Same when she has problems. The hard part
15   about defining friendship is that the word covers so much,
16   it can cover so many good things in a relationship. No
17   wonder its so hard to define.

Exercise 10-3:   Contrasting a draft and a finished version

DIRECTIONS: *The material below was a draft for a comparison/contrast paper. The student revised and polished his paper so that the final version was very different from this one. Read this version, underlining the sentences that you feel are weak in these respects:*

- *too vague and general*
- *illogical or rambling*
- *fragments or run-on sentences*
- *spelling, punctuation, or capitalization*

Then look at those passages in the revised version, noticing how the student changed the paper. The revised version is in Exercise 5-3 (pages 101–102).

1   I remember when I went on my first date. During
2   school I planned out how I wanted everything to go. All
3   from going up and asking her out to possibly getting that
4   good night kiss. First of all I went up to ask her and said
5   "Hi, I was just wondering if you would like to go out to a
6   movie or something on saturday?" Right away she said "yes."
7   So in turn I said "O.K. I will pick you up at eight."
8   Finally Saturday came. I picked her up at eight, and let me

9   tell you she looked great. We went to a little steak house

10   on the east side of town. The dinner we had was

11   spectacular. During dinner we discussed things such as what

12   movies we like and find out that we have many things in

13   common. After dinner we saw the best movie we had seen in a

14   long time. By the time the movie was over, it was pretty

15   late so I took her home. As I waked her to the door she

16   surprisingly gave me an unexpected kiss and said that she

17   would love to go out again sometime.

18   Then I felt a tap on my shoulder. It was my teacher,

19   she told me to stop daydreaming and do my work. I thought to

20   myself, I sure hope the date goes just as I dreamed. Well,

21   Saturday did come but nothing went as I planned. When I

22   picekd her up she was not ready, the food at the restaurant

23   was bad, we had nothing in common. Terrible movie, too.

24   When I brought her home I thought to myself it wasn't even

25   worth trying to get a kiss. As it turned out nothing went

26   as I planned.

Exercise 10-4:   Revising and proofreading your paragraph

DIRECTIONS: *Select one of the first paragraphs you wrote in this course. Revise and proofread it. Turn in your finished version and the original version. Use the exercise above and the finished version as a model.*

11

Writing Multiparagraph Units

Carrying Paragraph Principles into Longer Units

Most of what you have learned about writing paragraphs applies equally well to longer pieces of writing, such as magazine articles, reports, and essays. You will find, for example, that each multiparagraph unit is focused on a main idea, just as a good paragraph is focused on a topic idea. Moreover, the goal is the same: to give readers a clear, accurate understanding of the main idea. As you work with multiparagraph units, you will discover many other parallels between writing paragraphs and writing longer units.

Practice 11-1.   Reviewing principles of paragraph writing

DIRECTIONS: *Recall past chapters and answer these questions. What principles of paragraph writing have you learned?*

Add four items to this list:

1. Focus on a limited, manageable main idea.

2. Select relevant, specific support.

3. _____

4. _____

5. _____

6. _____

In Practice 11-1, you probably mentioned such concepts as support, development, coherence, and organization. All these principles guide you in writing paragraphs, and they will also guide you in writing multiparagraph documents, no matter what their length, topic, audience, or purpose.

Within a paragraph, each sentence has a distinct role. Typically, one is a topic sentence; others are supporting sentences, and one is a conclusion. Similarly, within the multiparagraph unit, each paragraph has a distinct role. Typically, one paragraph introduces the main idea of the entire unit, and several (or many) other paragraphs support that main idea. Additional paragraphs create transitions and summarize or restate the main idea.

Multiparagraph units can stand as self-contained pieces of writing, such as magazine articles. Or they can be parts of larger works, such as portions of chapters within books. Sometimes chapter sections are set apart with subheadings that indicate the main idea within each section. At other times, even when an author does not use subheadings, a multiparagraph unit of a chapter will explain a main idea.

For instance, author Isaac Asimov uses a multiparagraph passage in a chapter of *Fact and Fancy* to explain a main point. The chapter, entitled "My Built-in Doubter," shows that scientists must be skeptical about new ideas because they can easily be mistaken about the validity of those new ideas. Part of the way through the chapter, the author raises this question: "Can't one pick and choose and isolate the brilliant from the imbecilic, accepting the first at once and wholeheartedly, and rejecting the rest completely?"

In answer, Asimov presents a main idea that requires many paragraphs of explanation: "The godlike power to tell the good from the bad, the useful from the useless, the true from the false, instantly and *in toto* belongs to gods and not to men." To support that main idea, the author explains, uses details, gives examples, compares and contrasts ideas, raises and answers questions, then finally restates his main point:

an example to support a central idea

Let me cite you Galileo as an example; Galileo, who was one of the greatest scientific geniuses of all time, who invented modern science in fact, and who certainly experienced persecution and authoritarian enmity.

notice parallelism

establishes validity of Galileo as an example

Surely, Galileo, of all people, was smart enough to know a good idea when he saw it, and revolutionary enough not to be deterred by its being radical.

Well, let's see. In 1632 Galileo published the crowning work of his career, *Dialogue on the Two Principal Systems of the World* which was the very book that got him into real trouble before the Inquisition. It dealt, as the title indicates, with the two principal systems; that of Ptolemy,

fact

which had the earth at the center of the universe with the planets, sun and moon going about it in complicated systems of circles within circles; and that of Copernicus which had the sun at the center and the planets, earth, and moon going about *it* in complicated systems of circles within circles.

explains what Galileo accepted and rejected

Galileo did not so much as mention a *third* system, that of Kepler, which had the sun at the center but abandoned all the circles-within-circles jazz. Instead, he had the various planets traveling about the sun in ellipses, with the sun at one focus of the ellipse. It was Kepler's system that was correct and, in fact, Kepler's system has not changed in all the time that has elapsed since. Why, then, did Galileo ignore it completely?

rhetorical questions

Was it that Kepler had not yet devised it? No, indeed. Kepler's views on that matter were published in 1609, twenty-seven years before Galileo's book.

Parallelism in ¶ openings

Was it that Galileo had happened not to hear of it? Nonsense. Galileo and Kepler were in steady correspondence and were friends. When Galileo built some spare telescopes, he sent one to

Kepler. When Kepler had ideas, he wrote about them to Galileo.

a clear topic sentence

The trouble was that Kepler was still bound up with the mystical notions of the Middle Ages. He cast horoscopes for famous men, for a fee, and worked seriously and hard on astrology. He also

specific support in this ¶

spent time working out the exact notes formed by the various planets in creating the "music of the spheres" and pointed out that Earth's notes were mi, fa, mi, standing for misery, famine, and misery. He also devised a theory accounting for the relative distances of the planets from the Sun by nesting the five regular solids one within another and making deductions therefrom.

a transition into new ¶

Galileo, who must have heard of all this, and who had nothing of the mystic about himself, could only conclude that Kepler, though a nice guy and a bright fellow and a pleasant correspondent, was a complete nut. I am sure that Galileo heard all about the elliptical orbits and, considering the source, shrugged it off.

summary of previous ¶s

Well, Kepler was indeed a nut, but he happened to be luminously right on occasion, too, and Galileo, of all people, couldn't pick the diamond out from among the pebbles.

Shall we sneer at Galileo for that?

returning to main idea

Or should we rather be thankful that Galileo didn't interest himself in the ellipses *and* in astrology *and* in the nesting of regular solids *and* in the music of the spheres? Might not credulity have led him into wasting his talents, to the great loss of all succeeding generations?

restates main idea

No, no, until some supernatural force comes to our aid and tells men what is right and what is wrong, men must blunder along as best they can, and only the built-in doubter of the trained scientist can offer a refuge of safety.*

As the Asimov example illustrates, a multiparagraph passage uses the principles of unity, support, coherence, and logical organization, just as single paragraphs do. The same transitional words and phrases ensure coherence, and the same kinds of support are used as in individual paragraphs. In short, the similarities between individual paragraphs and longer passages greatly outnumber the differences.

The few differences between the two can be summed up in this way:

Paragraph	*Multiparagraph unit*
1. Uses a topic sentence.	Uses a thesis statement.
2. Supports its topic idea with other sentences.	Supports its thesis statement in a series of paragraphs.
3. Serves one purpose: to convey one main idea.	Different paragraphs serve different purposes: to introduce the thesis idea, to support the thesis idea, or to provide transitions or conclusions.

Most of your knowledge about the topic sentence applies equally well to a "thesis statement." Topic sentences and thesis statements are similar in these ways:

- They state the main idea in a piece of writing.
- They present and limit topics.
- They make assertions that must be supported.
- They often go beyond facts to express the writer's attitudes.

Two main differences distinguish topic sentences and thesis statements: scope and placement.

*New York: Doubleday, 1962, 189–190.

First, the thesis statement expresses a larger or more complicated idea that requires more extensive support. Consider Asimov's thesis statement again:

> The godlike power to tell the good from the bad, the useful from the useless, the true from the false, instantly and *in toto* belongs to gods and not to men.

That statement is too large, abstract, and complicated for one paragraph, but it can be explained and illustrated in many paragraphs.

Second, unlike the topic sentence (often placed first in the paragraph), a thesis statement is not likely to be the very first statement in a passage. A thesis statement is stated early in a multiparagraph unit, but it is not usually the very first sentence in an article, essay, or section within a book. More often, the thesis statement appears in the middle or at the end of the first paragraph.

In summary, if you looked at the skeleton of a paragraph, you would find something like this:

A paragraph

a topic sentence
   —a supporting idea
   —another supporting idea
   —another supporting idea
conclusion

You could find any number of supporting ideas, not necessarily three. Those support ideas could include details, examples, facts, and many other kinds of evidence.

If you looked at the skeleton of a multiparagraph document, you would see something like this:

A multiparagraph piece of writing

A paragraph that includes the thesis statement.
   —a supporting paragraph
      (with a topic sentence + supporting ideas)
   —a supporting paragraph
      (with a topic sentence + supporting ideas)
   —a supporting paragraph
      (with a topic sentence + supporting ideas)
A paragraph that summarizes or restates the thesis idea.

Here, too, you could have any number of supporting ideas, and that support could include details, examples, facts, and many other kinds of evidence.

Practice 11-2.   Analyzing differences between paragraphs and multiparagraph units

DIRECTIONS: *Compare and contrast the sketches above.*

1. What similarities do you see between the content of a paragraph and the content of a multiparagraph piece of writing?

   a. _____

   b. _____

   c. _____

2. What is the main difference?

   _____

   _____

   You found more similarities than differences in Practice 11-2 because the same principles apply in both instances. Though you may have answered question 2 in your own words, you probably said something about the scope, and therefore the length, of the writing.

   It is very difficult—indeed, impossible—to say exactly how much territory should be covered by a topic sentence or a thesis statement. Writers have to decide what they have to say, what the audience wants or needs to know, and what purpose is being served; however, scope and length are often influenced by assignments in school or guidelines at work.

   Take, for example, the general topic of love between a man and a woman. Thousands of writers have dealt with that topic. Just think of how many examples you have run into, counting song lyrics, poems, magazine articles, newspaper columns, nonfiction books, short stories, novels, plays, television programs, and movies. For every one, a writer had ideas to share; each writer used a main idea that reflected a special kind and amount of material.

   A student writer decided upon this thesis statement for an essay of several paragraphs: the love between a man and woman is shown in different ways at different stages in life. To support that thesis idea, the student wrote paragraphs about the romantic love of youth, the loyalty and devotion shown during the child-rearing years, and the tender caring of an aging spouse during later years.

   That student had to offer adequate support for the thesis statement by building strong individual paragraphs. Each paragraph needed a strong topic statement with support as well. A chronological arrangement of paragraphs was natural for that thesis. As often happens, the thesis statement suggests an orderly arrangement of ideas.

Here is one paragraph from the draft of that student's essay. Notice that it has a good topic sentence and an extended example for support:

[1]Mature love is shown by patience and tenderness. [2]Will and Sarah are good examples, and their lives prove that love can endure no matter what. [3]Sarah lives at a nursing home now, so they are separated for the first time in fifty-three years of marriage. [4]She is blind and paralyzed on the right side of her body, but Will visits her every day. [5]They talk about every detail that touches either of them. [6]He brings yellow carnations every Thursday because she always loved carnations, and yellow was her favorite color. [7]That she can't see them doesn't matter to him. [8]He feeds her, combs her hair, and reads to her every day, even if she seems sleepy or disinterested at times. [9]Will adores his wife and treats her with every kindness. [10]The frailty and sickness never change that for a moment.

Practice 11-3.   Analyzing a paragraph

DIRECTIONS: *Answer these questions about the paragraph above.*

1. Which is the topic sentence? _____

2. Which sentences provide support for the idea of patience without repeating the word "patience"?

   _____

3. Which sentences provide support for the idea of tenderness? _____

   _____

4. Which sentences are overly general and need more specific wording?

   _____

The paragraph preceding Practice 11-3 is one of several supporting paragraphs in an essay you will analyze in Exercise 11-1 at the end of the chapter. As that essay will show, each paragraph plays a role within a larger piece of writing. When you see a paragraph in isolation, as you did in Practice 11-3, it is impossible to see how it fits into a larger piece of writing. You can look again at the Isaac Asimov passage quoted above for further evidence of the same point: there, too, individual paragraphs have little meaning in isolation. But when you consider them in sequence, each one serves a purpose and makes sense within the larger context.

Creating Opening and Ending Paragraphs

Students often have a hard time getting started with their writing. After the first few lines, the ideas seem to flow, but getting those first few lines is often hard. In fact, students are not the only ones who find openings difficult; all writers face the same problem.

Naturally you want openings that arouse your readers' curiosity, making them want to read further. Good openings let readers know the topics and the controlling ideas; they do not make readers puzzle over the focus, purpose, or direction of the writing.

Though no one can prescribe the kinds of openings that will work for every purpose, you might consider the standard strategies listed below. If you experiment with them, you may find that these strategies work or that they lead you to other suitable openings:

- A striking fact or detail
  The detail must arouse curiosity or interest and point to what follows in the paper.

  Not this: A lot of sexual abuse goes on these days.
  or
  Frustration is a very unpleasant feeling.

  But this: During the time it takes to read this sentence, three people will be sexually abused.
  or
  You have only fifty cents on a hot, dry day, yet a can of cold soda pop costs fifty-five cents.

- A direct opening, setting the mood or scene
  The opening statements should be brief, specific, and original, not dull and too familiar. You want to set up a warm, inviting tone.

  Not this: Terminally ill people go through a lot of suffering.
  or
  I am going to tell about bigotry.

  But this: Until I was diagnosed with AIDS two years ago, I had no idea of the emotional distress suffered by terminally ill people.
  or

> I thought I understood racial bigotry: I wasn't a bigot, but I'd know bigotry when I saw it.

- An anecdote
  You can expand upon the previous strategy and use a brief narrative.

  Not this: I am going to tell about bigotry.
  > *or*

  I thought I understood racial bigotry: I'm not a bigot, but I'd know bigotry when I saw it.

  But this: During my trip to California last July, I stopped for a quick meal, never imagining what I was getting into. As soon as I walked into that pizza parlor and heard nothing but Spanish, I felt out of place. True, I had studied Spanish in school and could carry on a simple conversation. But for the first time in my memory, I was the minority person. I tried to look and act calm, but I was very uneasy. My understanding of racial bigotry began in that moment and has grown ever since.

- A quotation
  The quotation needs to be well worded, and it must pertain to the paper.

  Not this: "It ain't over 'til it's over," said Yogi Berra. (in a paragraph about musical performances)
  > *or*

  "If you have a perfect cast, a perfect director, and a rotten script, you've got a rotten movie," said Gene Wilder. (in a paper about dating)

  But this: "It ain't over 'til it's over," said Yogi Berra. (in a paragraph about trying hard in a piano contest)
  > *or*

  "If you have a perfect cast, a perfect director, and a rotten script, you've got a rotten movie," said Gene Wilder. (in a paper about the importance of good writing)

- A rhetorical question
  The question must lead into the topic, and it must be sharply focused to get your readers' interest. It must not be overly general, nor can it just dangle at the opening, only to be ignored as you write further.

  Not this: Isn't life something?
  > *or*

  What do you know about mountain climbing?

  But this: Have you ever stood by, helpless, while an infant floated face down in a pool?
  > *or*

  Who would have thought mountain climbing would take so much preparation?

Practice 11-4.   Improving weak openings

DIRECTIONS: *Revise these dull openings to make them more appealing to readers. Invent any details you need.*

1. Let me tell you about my daughter; she is pretty as a picture.

   _____

   _____

   _____

2. Let's talk about the environment.

   _____

   _____

   _____

3. Why is it that kids don't learn much in schools these days?

   _____

   _____

   _____

4. Poetry and what it has done for my life.

   _____

   _____

   _____

5. "I knew the record would hold until it was broken," is what our coach said about our winning streak.

   _____

   _____

   _____

Any of the strategies suggested above can be modified, combined, or discarded for something better. You can open in any way you wish, so long as you get the readers' interest, set the tone, and lead into your topic.

For a pleasing ending, you can use one of these strategies:

- a brief anecdote
- a quotation
- a restatement of the thesis idea, partly to reinforce that idea
- a summary of main points (particularly if the material is long or complicated)
- a repeat of a rhetorical question posed earlier, but now with an answer based on the discussion
- a reference to a detail, question, fact, or quotation used earlier

The last two possibilities make pleasing endings because they connect the ending with other parts of the paper. Connecting all parts of a multiparagraph unit is important, not just at the end, but from the title right on through the entire unit. The transitional words and phrases used within paragraphs can be used between paragraphs. You found one example in Exercise 5-3 (pages 101–102), and others appear in this chapter. You will also connect ideas by repeating key words and concepts throughout the multiparagraph unit. You found those connections in the Asimov passage, and you will see other examples in Exercise 11-1.

Practice 11-5. Examining openings and endings and internal connections

DIRECTIONS: *Look at a featured column in a magazine or newspaper. The column should consist of several paragraphs. Bring the column (or a copy of it) to class. Compare your findings with those of your classmates. Before class, answer these questions about the article you found.*

1. What column did you find? _____

_____

2. How did the writer begin? See if the writer used any of the strategies

mentioned in this chapter; if not, what was used? _____

_____

3. How did the writer end? _____

4. How did the ending relate to the rest of the column?

_____

_____

5. Find three examples of transitional words or phrases in the column and mark them on the original or the copy.

6. Overall, did this column get and hold your interest from beginning to end? _____

   If so, what got and held your interest? _____

   _____

   If not, which parts were dull or poorly presented?

   _____

   _____

In completing Practice 11-5, you probably found typical beginnings and endings used by writers. You may have discovered that some of the devices listed above for openings are also used as endings. Indeed, you should experiment with the items on that list as possible endings. You can use them individually or in combination.

When you write multiparagraph papers, you will devote a large part of your work to creating well-developed middle paragraphs. Naturally you will want each of them to support your thesis idea. You will work to organize those paragraphs logically, in a way suitable to your material. In many papers, you will organize according to the patterns you studied in previous chapters.

At the same time, remember to work for strong, appealing beginnings and appropriate endings. Extra effort at those two points makes your writing more satisfying for you and more pleasing to your readers.

Summary

- The principles of paragraph writing apply to longer pieces of writing: consider your audience and purpose, focus on a main idea, provide solid support and coherence, and organize logically.

- A thesis statement expresses the main point that a writer is making in the multiparagraph unit.

- Thesis statements can be broader and more complex than topic sentences because many paragraphs can be used for support.

- The opening paragraph in a multiparagraph unit attracts readers' attention and leads them into the topic. It often includes the thesis statement as well, most likely at the end of that paragraph.

- To start the opening paragraph, you might use a rhetorical question; a striking fact or detail; a direct statement setting the mood; an anecdote; a quotation; or any combination of these devices.

- The last paragraph should provide a graceful and satisfying ending. In it you can use the devices suggested for openings, restate the main idea, or summarize main points if the material is long or complicated.

- Writers of multiparagraph units connect paragraphs by using transitional words and phrases and by repeating key words and concepts.

- The main paragraphs of a multiparagraph unit support the thesis statement, but each is well developed in support of its own topic sentence as well.

Exercise 11-1:   Analyzing students' essays

DIRECTIONS: *Read the students' essays below and answer the questions that follow them. Lines are numbered for your convenience.*

Example A

1   What is the meaning of "love"? Many of us would have a
2   hard time thinking of a complete definition. We might try syn-
3   onyms like affection, admiration, devotion, respect, and enthu-
4   siasm, but none of those words is quite right. My view of love
5   has changed as I have grown up. Years ago, "love" was what I
6   felt about chocolate ice-cream cones. Now that I am older, I
7   save the word "love" for a powerful emotional bond between
8   people, especially a man and a woman. I have learned that the
9   love between a man and woman is shown in different ways at
10   different stages of life.

11   The first stage of a relationship is the romantic stage. I
12   can picture a young couple walking down a sandy beach. There
13   is a beautiful sunset, and the air is warm. The man turns to the
14   woman, takes her hand, and gently kisses the back of it. The
15   woman looks into his eyes, stands on her toes, and kisses him
16   on the forehead. Their affection is obvious, and they are lost in

17   their own world together. They talk softly about their feelings
18   and their future. It is a time for dreaming and planning.

19   Not long after the dreaming and planning stage, the
20   couple enters into the longest and busiest part of their rela-
21   tionship. They are married and building a life together. Dur-
22   ing these years, one or both of them are building careers. In
23   time, they may have children to rear, and if so, they are very
24   busy with helping children learn, grow, and develop into re-
25   sponsible citizens. The time passes quickly because every day is
26   so full. There is always the danger of losing sight of each other
27   because of the heavy demands of maintaining a job, a house-
28   hold, and the family. The main qualities of the relationship in
29   this stage are devotion and loyalty.

30   Then, as time passes, another stage is at hand. The chil-
31   dren are gone, and the couple's love is mature. Now patience
32   and tenderness are the main qualities. Will and Sarah are good
33   examples, and their lives prove that love can endure no matter
34   what. Sarah lives at a nursing home now, so they are separated
35   for the first time in fifty-three years of marriage. She is blind
36   and paralyzed on the right side of her body, but Will visits her
37   every day. They talk about every detail that touches either one
38   of them. He brings yellow carnations every Thursday because
39   she always loved carnations, and yellow was her favorite color.
40   That she can't see them doesn't matter to him. He feeds her,
41   combs her hair, and reads to her every day, even if she seems
42   sleepy or disinterested at times. Will adores his wife and treats
43   her with every kindness. The frailty and sickness never change
44   that for a moment.

45   I am not sure which stage is the "true love" mentioned in
46   songs and poetry. It seems to me that every stage is "true," and
47   each one has a kind of love that is precious. Love cannot be
48   static; it changes. I am sure that time brings differences, yet
49   a man and woman will find richness in their love all through
50   the years.

1. How does the writer try to arouse curiosity and generate interest in the

   topic? _____

   _____

   _____

2. How does the writer try to establish a warm, pleasant tone? _____

   _____

3. The opening paragraph leads to the thesis idea. Where is the thesis
   statement in that opening paragraph?

   _____

4. Three main paragraphs are used to support the thesis idea. Which of
   the three seems best developed with specific detail and examples?

   _____

   Explain why you think so. _____

   _____

5. Which of the three supporting paragraphs seems weakest, most gen-

   eral, and nonspecific? _____

6. In the paragraph you mentioned when answering question 5, what

   specific details might be used to improve the paragraph? _____

   _____

7. The writer connected the main paragraphs by using repetition of key
   words and concepts and by using transitions. Which key words or concepts do you find repeated?

   _____

   _____

Transitions can be found easily if you look at the end of one paragraph and the start of the next. In which lines do you find connections made by transitional words?

_____

_____

8. What is the topic sentence in the second paragraph? (Indicate by giving

    the line numbers.) _____

9. What is the topic sentence in the third paragraph? (Indicate by giving

    the line numbers.) _____

10. What is the topic sentence in the fourth paragraph? (Indicate by giving

    the line numbers.) _____

11. How did the writer connect the ending to the beginning? Be specific

    about words or concepts repeated or referred to. _____

    _____

    _____

12. Overall, what is the weakest part of this essay? How could the writer

    have improved it? _____

    _____

    _____

13. Overall, what is the strongest part of this essay?

    _____

    _____

14. Suggest a title for Example A. _____

    _____

Example B

1   I'm only twenty, and though I'm from a mostly white
2   community, I thought I understood about racial prejudice. I'm
3   no bigot, but I'd know bigotry when I saw it. It would be as
4   obvious as Archie Bunker saying "youse coloreds" on *All in the*
5   *Family.* As it turns out, I was only half right. I'm not a bigot,
6   and I never was. One day in California, though, I realized how
7   embarrassingly naive I was, and probably still am, about big-
8   otry in general.

9   Last month I was in a small town in California, where I
10   went into a pizza place to get some food. There was a pool table
11   in the corner, so to relax my nerves a little, I started shooting
12   some. After about five minutes of mostly practice shots, the
13   owner came over, watched a minute, and lit up a cigarette. I
14   asked if he was on break. He was. I asked if he cared to play a
15   game. He reached into his tomato-sauce-dirtied pants and
16   fished out a key. He then opened the pool table. It was really
17   nice of him to let me play for free the games we'd play together.

18   I thought he looked Hispanic, so I asked him, "¿Qué tal?"
19   which means "How's it going?" in Spanish. He looked at me
20   wide-eyed and asked me if I spoke Spanish. I did, and we chat-
21   ted for a while about who we were and why we were there, all
22   in Spanish. His name was Miguel. Now, this white guy speaking
23   Spanish didn't impress Miguel at all; they're pretty common in
24   the hot, arid part of California, which is where I was.

25   What really impressed him was my pool game. Now, I'm a
26   good player, and I've beaten some of the best at school (and
27   besides, this was one of those Tinker Toy, fifty-cents-a-game
28   tables). I'm used to the much bigger, regulation tables. But he
29   was gasping every time I made a tougher-than-average shot,
30   and we weren't playing for anything at all. He told me (all in
31   Spanish again) that I was better than anyone he'd seen and that
32   I should be at "Frankie's Billiards." (I changed the real name of
33   the place to protect the caulk-headed.) I said I thought about

34   going there, but it was on the other side of town, and the main
35   reason I came in was pizza, which still wasn't done. I asked him
36   why he didn't go in.
37   It was that simple; "¿Por qué no vas a Frankie's?" I asked
38   him. (That means "Why don't you go to Frankie's?") Innocent
39   question, right? I guess I didn't know that Hispanic people
40   weren't allowed in some establishments, that being one. He
41   told me that every time his brother Manuel and his friends
42   tried to enter, either they would tell them to leave, they'd be
43   beaten up by the other guys in there, or the management
44   would call the police and blame, oh, say, the pop stain on the
45   carpet, on them. There were no signs on the outside of the
46   building; that would be blatant discrimination. But any His-
47   panics who entered quickly got the message.
48   I thought this was pretty awful, but apparently Miguel
49   didn't. He was telling me this really calmly like he was reading a
50   menu or something. I asked him if that was typical of most
51   establishments. "Oh, sí," he replied. My pizza was ready and I
52   had to take off, but I thanked Miguel for the games, and he
53   thanked me for chatting with him. It really is a shame that the
54   next white boy he sees will probably either beat him up or rip
55   him off, if Frankie's is any indication. As for me, I'm by no
56   means worldly wise or anything like that, but I think I know a
57   little bit more about bigotry than I did before.

1. How does the writer try to arouse curiosity and generate interest in the

   topic? _____

   _____

   _____

2. How does the writer try to establish a warm, pleasant tone? _____

   _____

   _____

3. The opening paragraph leads to the thesis idea. Where is the thesis statement in that opening paragraph?

_____

4. Four main paragraphs are used to support the thesis idea. Which of the four seems best developed, with specific details and examples?

_____

_____

5. Which of the four supporting paragraphs seems weakest, most general, and nonspecific? _____

6. In the paragraph you mentioned when answering question 5, what specific details might be used to improve the paragraph? _____

_____

_____

7. The writer connected the main paragraphs by using repetition of key words and concepts and by using transitions. Which key words or concepts do you find repeated?

_____

_____

Transitions can be found easily if you look at the end of one paragraph and the start of the next. In which lines do you find connections made by transitional words?

_____

_____

8. What is the topic sentence in the second paragraph? (Indicate by giving the line numbers.) _____

9. What is the topic sentence in the third paragraph? (Indicate by giving the line numbers.) _____

10. What is the topic sentence in the fourth paragraph? (Indicate by giving the line numbers.) _____

11. How did the writer connect the ending to the beginning? Be specific about words or concepts repeated or referred to. _____

_____

_____

12. Overall, what is the weakest part of this essay? How could the writer have improved it? _____

_____

_____

13. Overall, what is the strongest part of this essay?

_____

_____

_____

14. Suggest a title for Example B. _____

_____

Exercise 11-2:   Writing a multiparagraph unit

DIRECTIONS: *Expand one of your best paragraphs into a multiparagraph unit. That unit could be an essay, a memo, a business or personal letter, a report, or any other document you prefer. Form a thesis statement that sums up the point of your writing, and use several paragraphs to support that thesis idea.*

Bring your paper to class for peer evaluation. The questions in Exercise 11-1 can be adapted for use during your analysis of papers.

Appendix **A**

Manuscript Form

1. Your papers should be typed or word processed. Use good-quality paper, not erasable paper that smudges easily.

2. If you cannot type, write with dark ink on lined tablet paper or looseleaf paper. Do not use spiral notebook paper. Wide-lined paper is preferable.

3. If you have a title, center it at the top. Capitalize the main words of the title. Do not underline the title. Individual paragraphs do not require titles, but if you want to add a title, you may.

4. Write on one side of the paper only.

5. Indent the first line of a paragraph five spaces or about a half inch.

6. Double-space your work. Make last-minute corrections, using a pen, between the lines or in the margins.

7. Leave margins of about an inch on the left and right sides. Use about an inch and a half at the top and the bottom.

8. Write your name at the top right corner of each page.

9. If you have more than one page, number the pages and staple them. Do not crimp the corners.

10. Do not fold the papers unless your teacher directs you to do so.

Appendix **B**

Correction Symbols

Symbol	Explanation	Example
sp	Spelling	mispelled (correct: misspelled) *sp*
⌐⌐	Two words	a lot (correct: a lot)
⌣	One word	week end (correct: weekend)
CS	Comma splice	I went home, then I wrote my paper. *cs*
fused	Fused sentence	I went home then I wrote my paper. *fused*
frag	Sentence fragment	When I wrote my paper. *frag*
num	Spell out	The bear stole *three* 8 picnic baskets. *num*
ab	Explain or write out the words	The *captain* cpt gave us orders.

Symbol	Explanation	Example
dang. mod.	Dangling modifier	~~Driving~~ When Jim was driving down the street, the bike turned over.
mis. mod.	Misplaced modifier	My friend and I ⋏cleaned the kitchen. ~~with my friend.~~
no comp.	No comma (one subject + a compound verb)	The game was close⁄ *omit comma* and finally ran into another inning.
intro	Set off an introductory element	After the tenth inning, *Comma needed* the home team had won.
Shift	Shift in person (often to *you*, second person)	Carpentry is a hard job, requiring a lot of ~~you.~~ *carpenters.*
pron	Incorrect pronoun usage	The gift was given to him and ~~I.~~ *me*
order	Incorrect order	The gift was given to ~~me and him.~~ *him and me*
agr	Subject/verb agreement	A cast of nine actors ~~were~~ needed for *was* that play.
⟨.”⟩	Correct order of marks used	He said, "Hell⟨o”.⟩ (correct: .")
⟨.”⟩	Correct order of marks used	After he said, "hell⟨o”,⟩ Mike walked into the room. (correct: "hello,")

Symbol	Explanation	Example
cap	Capital letter needed	I asked ~~dad~~ *Dad* for the car keys to drive to West High School for the game.
/	No capital letter needed	I asked my ~~D~~*dad*ad for the car keys to drive to the high school for the game.
⌣'or ⌣	Use apostrophe or omit apostrophe	Mother(')s car, her() car
e	Delete word or symbol	The sentence is i~~s~~ mistyped.
//ism	Parallelism	
punct	Punctuation error	
dict	Diction (word choice)	
¶	Paragraph	
¶s	paragraphs	
¶ing	paragraphing	

Index

Credits *(continued)*